ANALOG IN, DIGITAL OUT

BRENDAN DAWES ON INTERACTION DESIGN

New Riders

VOICES THAT MATTER™

Analog In, Digital Out:
Brendan Dawes on Interaction Design

New Riders
1249 Eighth Street
Berkeley, CA 94710
510/524-2178
800/283-9444
510/524-2221 (fax)

Find us on the Web at: www.newriders.com

To report errors, please send a note to errata@peachpit.com

New Riders is an imprint of Peachpit, a division of Pearson Education

Senior Executive Editor: Marjorie Baer
Development Editor: Camille Peri
Production Editor: Susan Rimerman
Design: Charlene Charles-Will
Composition: Kim Scott, Bumpy Design
Cover Design and Photographs: Brendan Dawes

All interior photographs by Brendan Dawes unless otherwise indicated.

ISBN 0-321-42916-8

9 8 7 6 5 4 3 2 1

Printed and bound in the United States of America

Acknowledgments

The book would not have been possible without the help of the following people:

Camille Peri, my patient editor, whose support, suggestions, and guidance during this little journey pushed me into creating something I'm very proud of.

The incredible design and production team—production editor Susan Rimerman, design manager Charlene Will, and especially compositor Kim Scott—for making sense of this thing that was in my head and turning it into a beautiful visual reality.

Senior executive editor Marjorie Baer, for her sage advice, and for believing in this project and letting me make the book I've always wanted to make.

Executive marketing manager Damon Hampson, my fellow northerner, for convincing me that I might have something interesting to say (occasionally). I hope that still holds true.

All the incredible people at magneticNorth—for never letting me get too big for my boots, even though I keep telling them working with me is like winning a prize every day! To Lou Cordwell and Janet Harrison, I just want to say thanks for giving me the opportunity to help shape this little family we call mN.

Finally, my wife, Lisa, without whom none of this would have been possible. Thanks for being my co-pilot in this continuing big-smiley adventure. There is indeed "no place like home."

Contents

INTRODUCTION

Running with Scissors

I remember it as if it were yesterday. It's one of those things you never really forget. I had just been onstage, talking about this and that at a Flashforward conference in New York, when a young lady came up to me and said, "Gee, Brendan, you're like a big thought lozenge. I could suck on you all day!"

"I could suck

I explained that, while I was very flattered, for practical reasons at the very least, I'd have to give that one a miss.

Me, a *thought lozenge*? My mum would be proud! My teachers would be shocked! After all, I was the kid who stared out the window in class. I was the one whose school reports seemed to have been preprinted to read: "Must try harder." Now here I was, standing on a stage in New York City, being compared to some kind of inspirational boiled sweet. So I got to thinking: Hey, why should this woman have all the fun? Why not spread the sweets around? In fact, forget the sweets—let's make a book! A book that is an eclectic mix of thoughts, projects, anecdotes, and observations about my approach to interaction design.

So let's get something out of the way right now: I'm an uneducated bloke with not a single qualification to my name. Consequently these pages don't reference academic research, user testing, or any of that malarkey. While those things are incredibly important, that's not what this book is about. It is simply about some of my experiences and ideas—from more than ten years of working with interactive media, but also from all the way back to when I was growing up. If you want a book that is full of big words, that will impress people at parties, then "please move along, there's nothing to see here."

This is a book about diving in headfirst. No long-winded pontifications. Let's just make stuff! Stuff that challenges convention and takes risks. Stuff that is just plain fun. I've always liked taking things apart, questioning how they work and seeing if I can screw them up, for want of a better expression—whether I'm mashing up movies or making Google pretty unusable just for the hell of it. Forget manuals. Let's just turn this thing on, press some buttons, and see what it can do.

Photo by Lisa Brammah-Dawes

My guiding philosophical question is:
Why does it have to be like that?

What would I do

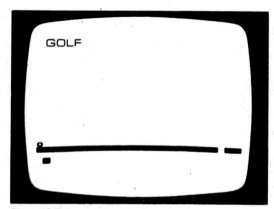

GOLF

Play golf. Estimate your drive force
on the fairway.

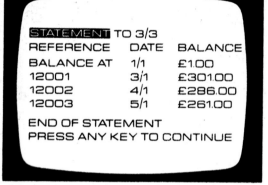

STATEMENT TO 3/3		
REFERENCE	DATE	BALANCE
BALANCE AT	1/1	£1.00
12001	3/1	£301.00
12002	4/1	£286.00
12003	5/1	£261.00

END OF STATEMENT
PRESS ANY KEY TO CONTINUE

*Flummox your Bank Manager by keeping
your finances at your finger tips.

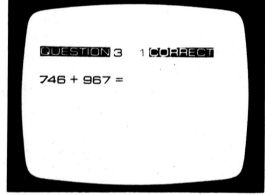

QUESTION 3   1 CORRECT

746 + 967 =

Teach the children maths from
Division to Volume.

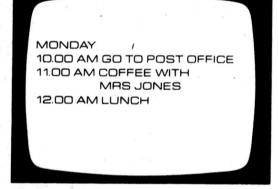

MONDAY
10.00 AM GO TO POST OFFICE
11.00 AM COFFEE WITH
              MRS JONES
12.00 AM LUNCH

*Keep a diary of future appointments
and past events.

?

Or within a week you can write your own
complex programs.

How to program
the ZX81

All you need to know for £14.95.

with a computer?

*Keep the rundown on friends, everything from their telephone numbers to birthdays.

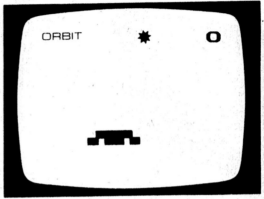

Play Orbit and captain a spacecraft.

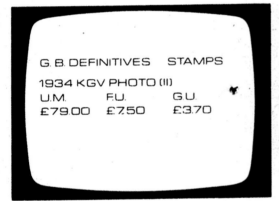

*Catalogue all your collections from coins to stamps.

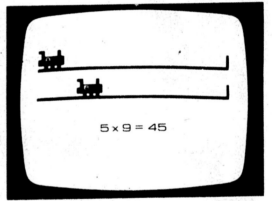

*Teach the children multiplication and play trains at the same time.

And a great range of books ....

.... and magazines to help you become an expert.

That's pretty much been my philosophy and my approach to programming and design since I got my first computer in 1981—a Sinclair ZX81, with 16K of RAM, replete with no sound or color. The thing I love about that computer, even now, is that you simply switched it on; it booted up instantly and then just sat there with a cursor blinking on and off, as if to say, "Come on then, do something."

When I finally figured out how to "do something"—a simple program that would fill the screen with a word or two—I went into my local electronics shop, which happened to have a few ZX81s set up, and made the word *arse* fill the screen as I left the store. Yes, it was very juvenile, but what do you expect? I was a juvenile (16 years old) and I hated that store.

It was my own little protest about the bad service I had often received there. This was power! It was a public forum that allowed me to have my say before the Web came along. You might say it was my first public installation.

Have I grown up since then? Not really. In fact, I may be getting "worse" as I get older. I mean that the rebellious, curious spirit that made me twist the message on those screens in that store still lives on in some form or another in the work that I and the design team I work with produce at magneticNorth, in the U.K. Fundamentally our guiding philosophical question is: Why does it have to be like that?

When I look back on the sort of things I've created, I've always been driven by a thirst for both ripping things apart and getting a reaction from people. For a short while before getting into digital design, around 1990, I was into DJ mixing, and eventually I cut a couple of records back at the height of the U.K. rave scene. It was really important to me (as it still is) to get people to see/hear/touch the stuff that I made. So getting a record deal was something I'll never forget. (Remember, this was pre-Web, pre-MP3.) What's the point of making things if only *you* can enjoy them? You need to see how people react to your creations, whether they are Web sites, interactive installations, or dance records.

Sinclair ZX81 Personal Computer—the heart of a system that grows with you.

Kit: £49.⁹⁵

Built: £69.⁹⁵

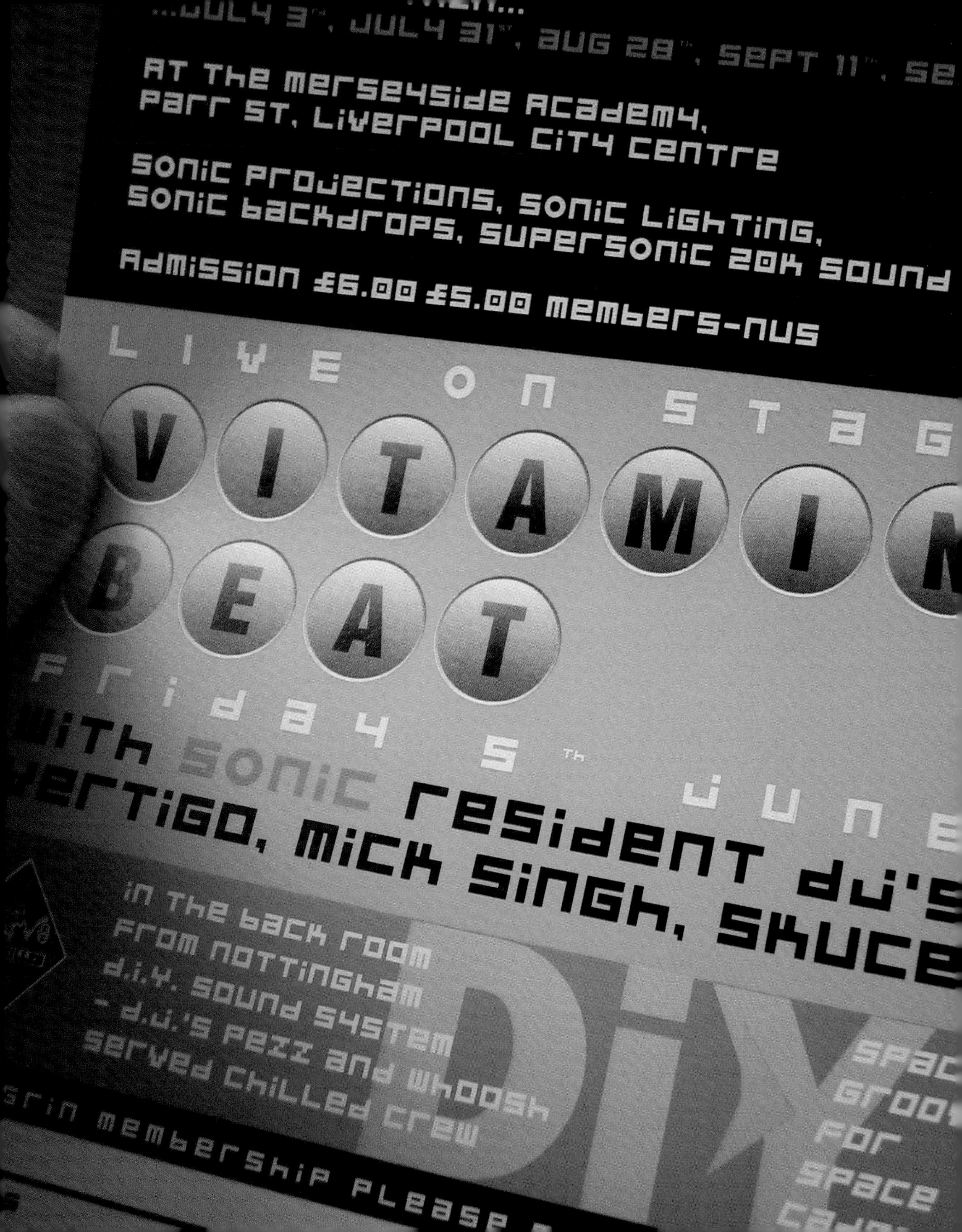

...JULY 3RD, JULY 31ST, AUG 28TH, SEPT 11TH, SE

AT THE MERSEYSIDE ACADEMY,
PARR ST, LIVERPOOL CITY CENTRE

SONIC PROJECTIONS, SONIC LIGHTING,
SONIC BACKDROPS, SUPERSONIC 20K SOUND

ADMISSION £6.00 £5.00 MEMBERS-NUS

LIVE ON STAGE

VITAMIN
BEAT

FRIDAY 5TH

JUNE

WITH SONIC

VERTIGO, MICK SINGH, SKUCE

RESIDENT DJ'S

IN THE BACK ROOM
FROM NOTTINGHAM
D.I.Y. SOUND SYSTEM
- DJ'S PEZZ AND WHOOSH
SERVED CHILLED CREW

DIY

SPAC
GROO
FOR
SPACE
CA

FOR MEMBERSHIP PLEASE

So think of this book as a starting point, a means to the end of not just thinking in new ways, but also of creating in new ways. A toolkit to help you make more dynamic work and get it out into the wider world, inspired by that world around you. The logic may challenge you: photos of cheese, next to dynamically generated art, next to stories about origami swans left on trains, next to chunks of code. It's my take on things—one that I hope will inspire, anger, bemuse, amuse, and provoke you. Most of all, I hope it will make you look at the world around you, both analog and digital, in a new way.

Brendan Dawes
On a train heading towards Manchester
July 2006

MODERN CLASS

THE PHANT
TOLLBO

1

Looking Up

Pretty much every day, I get the train into the center of Manchester along with hundreds of other commuters. Call me stupid, but for a long time I refused to buy a weekly train ticket because I didn't want to become "part of the system," even though it would save me around £10 a week. I didn't want to become like the commuters whose sole purpose seems to be getting from point A to point B in the shortest amount of time, whilst ignoring everything around them. But eventually I succumbed to the idea of saving a bit of money and avoiding the hassle of buying a ticket every day.

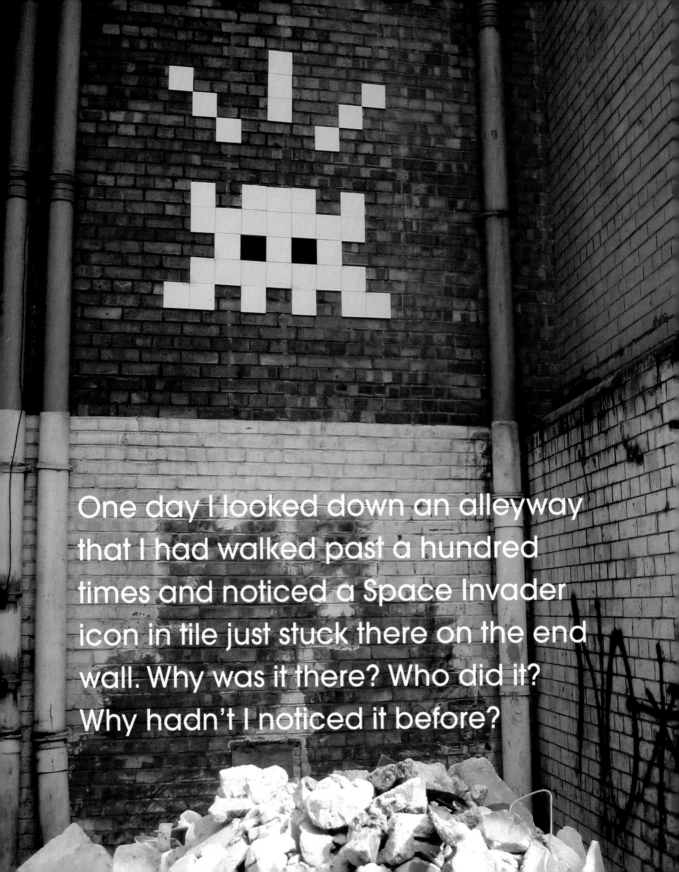

One day I looked down an alleyway that I had walked past a hundred times and noticed a Space Invader icon in tile just stuck there on the end wall. Why was it there? Who did it? Why hadn't I noticed it before?

Even though I am now part of the System, so to speak, I am still determined to avoid getting drawn into a "default" view of my journey to and from work, as there's always something to be discovered. For instance, one day I looked down an alleyway that I had walked past a hundred times and noticed a Space Invader icon in tile just stuck there on the end wall. Why was it there? Who did it? Why hadn't I noticed it before?

It's very easy to put your head down and not notice what's around you. You and I do it all the time. This phenomenon is crystallized in a book I picked up while on holiday in Spain. Usually in Spanish supermarkets, the selection of books in English is pretty poor—all Jeffrey Archer, Dan Brown, and Jackie Collins. In my frustration, I had a look at what the children's section had to offer. I came across *The Phantom Tollbooth*, by Norton Juster. It's not new—in fact it's a children's classic—but it was new to me.

The whole book is just a fantastic read, full of imagination, but one passage really stuck with me. The lead character comes across a town that has completely disappeared. The buildings are still there, but they're invisible to everyone who lives there. Why? Because the people are so engrossed in getting as quickly as possible from A to B, everything in between has simply disappeared. Because they don't bother to look up anymore, the world around them faded away, unneeded by the people.

In a sense, this happens to you, me, and everyone else every day of the week. I don't mean just that we forget to notice the beautiful buildings around us. I mean that sometimes it is far too easy to live our lives in "default setting"—doing what we know, what we feel comfortable with. It's much more difficult to stop, look up, and ask ourselves: Is there another way? Is there an alternative?

Quite often at magneticNorth, I interview prospective team members who seem to have a default response when I ask them where they draw their inspiration. The first thing they usually do is trot out a load of design portal sites and then follow that up by mentioning a trendy design bookstore like Magma. While Web sites and books are indeed useful and undoubtedly add to the mix of stuff that goes into their heads in the hope of making something original, they're only ever part of the story. I mean, if you're designing for the Web, why look at loads of design portals that show loads of Web sites that essentially all look the same? And ditto for bookshops that just sell design books. Surely they offer too narrow a view to be really inspirational.

I need to be more extreme. So much so that I
purposefully go out of my way not to visit either
Web sites or design bookstores that often. In their
place, I try to open my eyes to other things around
me. I'm not talking here about visiting pretentious
art galleries or watching a million foreign films—I'm
talking about opening my eyes to the things that
exist in everyday life. Personally I find what goes
on in popular culture far more interesting than the
stuff that other people deem to be "cool." I'd much
rather visit a supermarket than an art gallery, and
watch how people interact with the space and the
products there. Even the boring journey to work
can reveal insights that you and I can use in our
design work—as I will show elsewhere in this book.

So every day I try and force myself to "look up"—to open my mind to the world of input that constantly surrounds us.

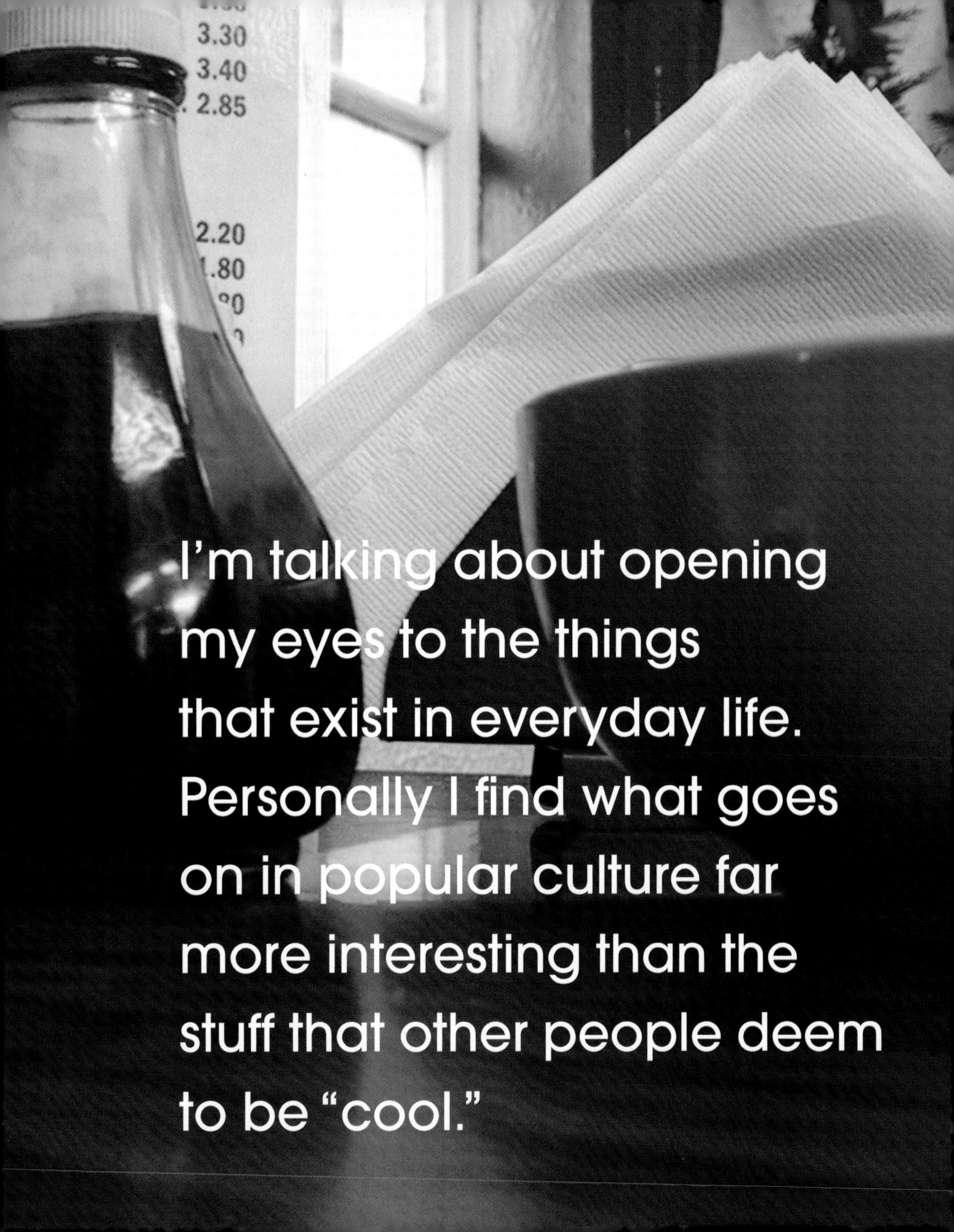

3.30
3.40
. 2.85

2.20
1.80
°0

I'm talking about opening my eyes to the things that exist in everyday life. Personally I find what goes on in popular culture far more interesting than the stuff that other people deem to be "cool."

Revolutionaries: The Zephyr Skateboard Team

Revolutionaries: The Zephyr skateboard team, immortalized in the documentary Dogtown and Z-Boys, changed the world of skateboarding in one fell swoop. Skateboarding was never the same once these guys came onto the scene with their daredevil moves and don't-give-a-shit attitude. They simply wouldn't conform to the way people thought you should skate. They made their own rules—and either you got it or you didn't. In the process, they mutated surfing style with skating style to create a whole new art form. Check out the film on DVD and this Web site for more information: http://skateboard.about.com/od/boardscience/a/DogtownHistory.htm

Revolutionaries: The Zephyr skateboard team, immortalized in the documentary Dogtown and Z-Boys, changed the world of skateboarding in one fell swoop. Skateboarding was never the same once these guys came onto the scene with their daredevil moves and don't-give-a-shit attitude. They simply wouldn't conform to the way people thought you should skate. They made their own rules—and either you got it or you didn't. In the process, they mutated surfing style with skating style to create a whole new art form. Check out the film on DVD and this Web site for more information: http://skateboard.about.com/od/boardscience/a/DogtownHistory.htm

Hi Honey!

Downloads

2

Just Ring the Bell When You Get There

As I'm sitting here beginning to write, the doorbell rings. Not the doorbell for my front door—the one for my Web site. When a visitor hits the homepage of my site, a real doorbell chime gets triggered on my desk. It's as if the visitor were saying, "Hello, just called to say 'hi.'"

Why, you ask, would I have such a thing? It began when I wanted to represent a user's visit to my site in a way that didn't require me to visit a specific statistics page. After all, I already have a really great log file page that tells me everything I want to know and loads of stuff I didn't know I want to know. I was looking for something beyond a software application that lights up and fires up a message on screen. I wanted a real-time, real-world notification that someone was dropping in, even when I was not looking at the screen or even near the computer. What better way, I thought, than to rig up an actual doorbell chime?

As always with a project like this, I sketch out how I can make it work. First there was the chime itself and the issue of getting it triggered by my Macintosh rather than by a push button wired to the chime. This is where the brilliant Teleo interface module would come in. But the trickier bit was figuring out how to send a message from my homepage to the chime. What I needed was software that could register the user's "appearance" on the site and get that to trigger the chime. Easy! Multi-user chat server. Chat server? Doorbells? Read on.

Hi Honey!

Downloads

When the chimes sound, it makes me think, *There's someone on my site right now.* A real person. And that's kind of nice.

First I stopped by the local do-it-yourself hardware shop and picked up the required doorbell—nothing fancy, just a simple two-chime affair. At home I put in the batteries and wired the provided bell wire to the terminals inside the chime. Touching the wires together at the other end made it chime. I just needed to get my Mac to connect the wires. I just needed Teleo.

The Teleo module is a great piece of hardware made by Making Things. It allows you to interface with the real world through Flash, Max/MSP, and C++ via a Universal Serial Bus (USB) lead. In a nutshell, you can attach switches and sensors to the Teleo, which can then control things inside a Flash movie; conversely, you can have Flash control motors, lights, and in this case a doorbell that are connected to the Teleo. On this project, I needed to use it very simply—to send a signal from a Flash movie on my Mac to the Teleo, which would then make a connection to the two wires from the door chime, which would then make the bell sound.

I connected one wire to one of the Digital Out sockets and the other to the ground (GND) socket. Then I needed to create a piece of code that would make the chime trigger. Fortunately, that is very simple to do using Teleo. I created a little Flash movie that contained one button and then added this piece of code:

```
import com.makingthings.*;
var dout : TIntroDout = new TIntroDout(0);
dout.setValue( false );
dout0_btn.onRollOver = function() {
    dout.setValue(true);
}
dout0_btn.onRollOut = function() {
    dout.setValue(false);
}
```

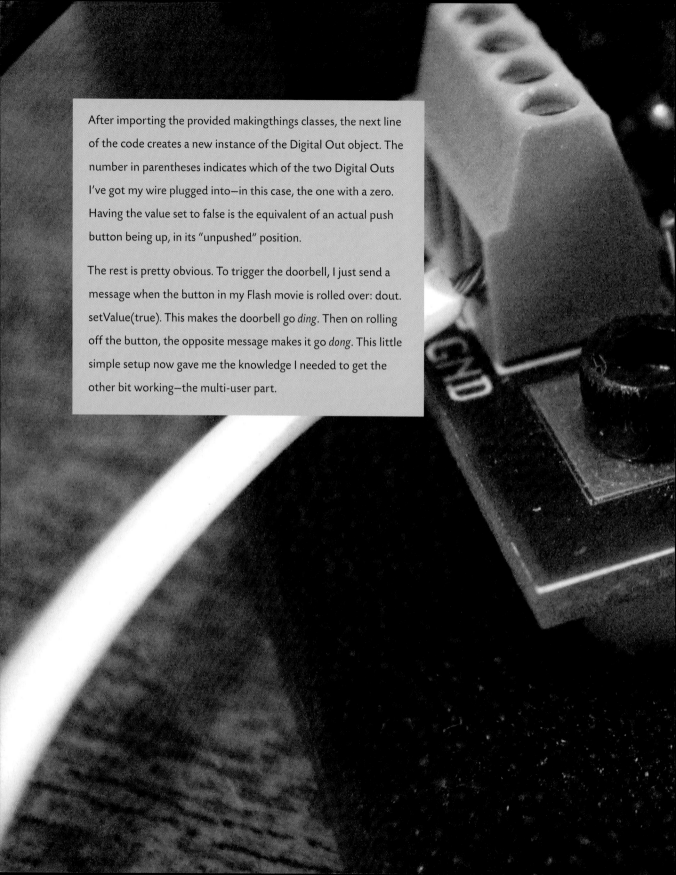

After importing the provided makingthings classes, the next line of the code creates a new instance of the Digital Out object. The number in parentheses indicates which of the two Digital Outs I've got my wire plugged into—in this case, the one with a zero. Having the value set to false is the equivalent of an actual push button being up, in its "unpushed" position.

The rest is pretty obvious. To trigger the doorbell, I just send a message when the button in my Flash movie is rolled over: dout. setValue(true). This makes the doorbell go *ding*. Then on rolling off the button, the opposite message makes it go *dong*. This little simple setup now gave me the knowledge I needed to get the other bit working—the multi-user part.

My idea was to have a small, inconspicuous Flash movie on my homepage that simply looks like an image. Though it appears not to do anything, it would actually log the user into the chat server. I would have the same Flash movie running on my Mac, but mine also had the functionality for the door chime. So the Flash movie would log onto the chat server, waiting for users to "log in." When they did, my Flash movie would see them and I'd hear *ding-dong*.

Did I write a chat server for this specific purpose? Why reinvent the wheel? I used Colin Moocks' excellent Unity chat server. I didn't even need to write reams of code to create a client. I simply hacked up Colin's USimpleChat example, basically just ripping out the bits I didn't need. In no time, I had my weird doorbell gizmo thing up and running.

Now when the chimes sound, it actually makes me think, *There's some-one on my site right now. A real person.* And that's kind of nice. There's now a little bit of interaction—admittedly one way—between a user and me. Of course, having the chime on all the time could indeed drive a person crazy. But the concept has a lot of scope. You don't need to use a doorbell. You could use a light or a servo (motor you can turn to any angle) or something that inflates larger with each visit. If you want to create something like this, you'll know where you want to go with it.

Helpful Sites

Interface the real world simply and cheaply with Flash, Max, and C++ using fantastic pieces of hardware from Making Things, at

www.makingthings.com.

Colin Moock's great Java-based multi-user server,

www.moock.org/unity.

3

"Brown Paper and String" Moments

I own a digital watch that is, on the face of it, a ridiculous design for a device with the sole purpose of telling the time. Other watches get straight to the point. We look at them, they tell us the time, we're finished, thank you, goodnight. Yet this watch—well, it requires some work.

This watch requires that I use my other hand to get it to reveal itself: I must press the button on the side to get the current time. Wholly inefficient, compared to most other watches. Surely no one would want a device that requires more effort to use? Surely this would be a commercial disaster? Of course not. Why? Because we're humans, full of "flaws" like emotions and taste. We're not machines that make decisions based simply on efficiency.

I actually bought this watch for the experience of using it. It's just much more stimulating to use than other watches and, more importantly, it's more enjoyable. It looks, to me anyway, better than any other watch I know, and when other people see it they want to touch it because it is far more interesting than your standard time-telling devices.

To my mind, that's because we crave experiences. It's the experience of an object, the little special details, which make us want to interact with it in some way, physically or emotionally. This is particularly evident when making purchasing decisions, something that logic would suggest should always be guided by price.

Surely no one would want a device that requires more effort to use? Surely this would be a commercial disaster? Of course not.

Of course, we know that that is not the case at all. There are many different considerations going through our minds when we choose to part with our hard-earned cash—this is what branding is all about. But I think the decision can usually be brought back to how we experience the product, even when buying something as mundane as cheese.

Even though it is just a block of cheese, there's a brand experience contained in the small details of how it's presented.

It does for me anyway. Here's some cheese I bought from the "top people's store," Harvey Nichols. While the cheese does indeed taste lovely, to be honest it would taste just as good from a store down the road that sells it at a lower price. But look at the experience of getting to the product.

First, there's the beautiful wax bag, not some cheap paper or plastic thing. It reminds me of when we used to have family-owned corner cheese shops. Then the cheese itself is wrapped in high-quality paper that just feels great in my hands and gets my mind thinking, This is a bit special. The finishing touch is the Harvey Nichols sticker that seals the wrapper—not a gummy cash-register price tag slapped onto plastic wrap but a specially designed label with the sole job of sealing food wrapped in paper. These little elements combine to suggest that this product is a cut above the rest, that cheese bought from this store is a premium thing.

All that wrapping pleases me because someone somewhere has designed that experience—and yet it's only cheese! But now the act of eating the cheese is not solely about the process of eating; it is wrapped in an overall experience that makes it much more interesting.

The actual process of getting to the end, the journey to the goal, is what makes being there a much more special experience.

Then there is my favorite bookshop, a true antiquarian bookseller that has managed to stay alive despite giant competition. I could buy books from less-expensive places and, while I do buy many books online, when I can I buy my books from this very special place. All because I love the experience of buying a book there.

As soon as you step in, you feel that the shop itself is a place of wonder. Impossibly high shelves are stacked to the ceiling with stories and knowledge. A little winding staircase takes you up to three tightly cramped floors filled everywhere you look with books in old bookcases. As you climb, you feel that you're on some kind of

adventure, as if you've stumbled upon a secret passage to a literary discovery. But what I really love about this place is what happens when you buy a book there.

Rather than simply put your book in a bag, as the clerks do at nearly every other bookshop, the booksellers wrap it in brown paper using a hand-built paper-wrapping gizmo—a roll of brown paper stuck to the wall—and then they tie it up with string. Wow. Suddenly this book is something special: a kind of gift to be unwrapped rather than hauled out of a generic bag. It seems almost magical.

The experience of the book becomes a special user journey simply by adding some brown paper and string.

The three experiences that I've described share a common characteristic. The actual process of getting to the end, the journey to the goal, is what makes being there a much more special experience.

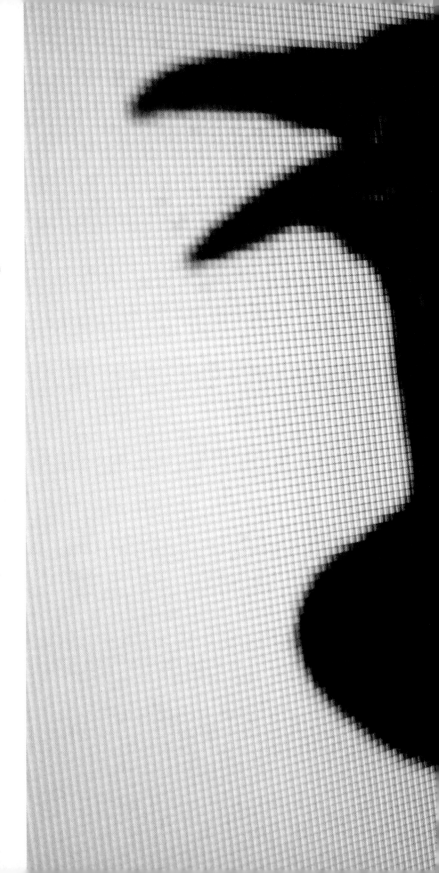

You can apply this concept to your work, even in small ways. Take, for example, a piece I made for a BD4D event in London. BD4D, which stands for "By Designers For Designers," is a sort of creative movement started by designers Ryan Carson and Ryan Shelton. Every few months they put on free events all over the world with the sole aim of sharing and celebrating creativity. At each event, there are a handful of featured "creatives," who usually make something and then talk about what it is and how they made it. I wanted to present a timeline of Alfred Hitchcock films in a much more interesting way than simply as a list. I wanted an extra experiential layer that added to the whole experience.

Borrowing from Hitchcock's *The Birds,* I used birds sitting on an abstract telephone wire to represent his films. When the piece begins, the birds fly in and land on the wire, and you can see all of Hitchcock's works by rolling over them with your mouse. But the little extra bit of detail—that "brown paper and string" moment—comes when you select a decade or a certain actor. The birds that represent the irrelevant films fly away, leaving those related to your selection on the wire. It is a simple, atmospheric touch that makes the request for information a mini-journey in itself, heightening your expectancy a bit as you wait for the final revelation. Of course, like a wristwatch that simply tells time, I could have made this straightforward, no-nonsense information retrieval. But I believe that doing it this way was more involving and, well, more fun.

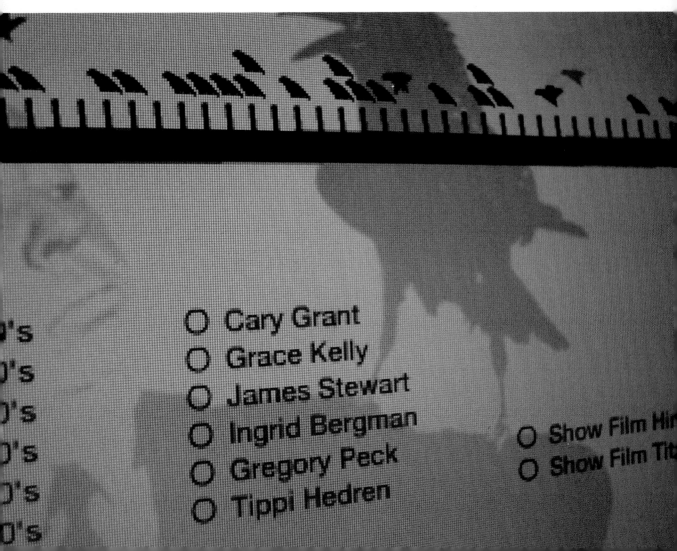

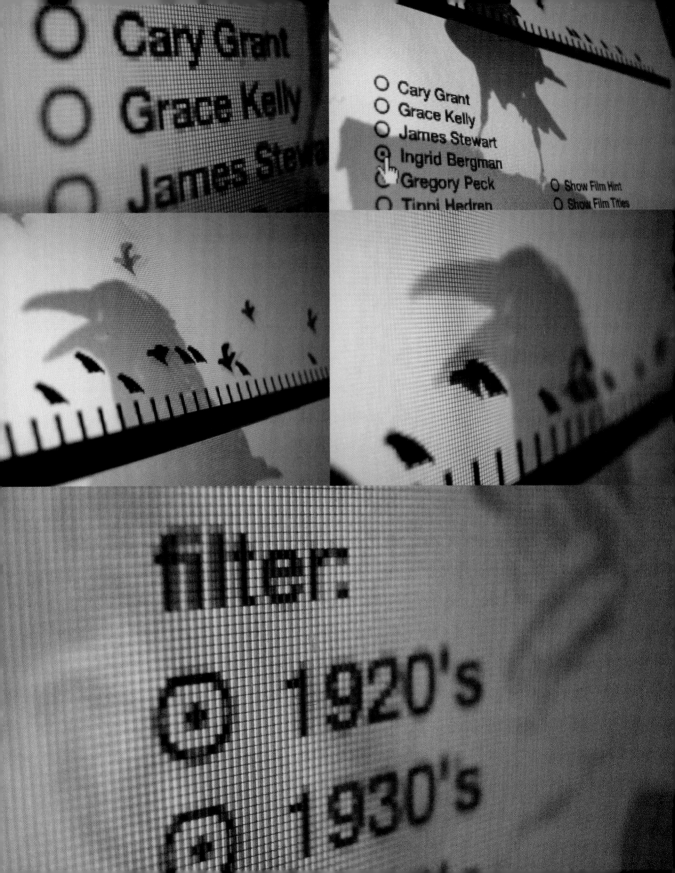

Cary Grant
Grace Kelly
James Stewart

○ Cary Grant
○ Grace Kelly
○ James Stewart
◉ Ingrid Bergman
○ Gregory Peck
○ Tippi Hedren

○ Show Film Hint
○ Show Film Titles

filter:

◉ 1920's

◉ 1930's

4

Play-Doh as Interface

In 2004 HOW magazine asked me to do a session at the annual HOW Design Conference, which would be held in Chicago the next year. I immediately said yes, as I'd never done the HOW conference and Chicago was somewhere I'd always wanted to visit.

EVERY IS NU

Several months before the conference, the sponsors needed a session description from me—something that was about interaction design but was a bit unusual, that would have people talking after the session. I already knew that the crux of the session was going to be about alternative interfaces and such, but I really needed to do something so different that it would stick in people's minds.

As I typed away at home, I looked around the room until my eyes came to rest on a tub of Play-Doh. That's it. I'll use Play-Doh as an interface. Yeah, cool. Come again?

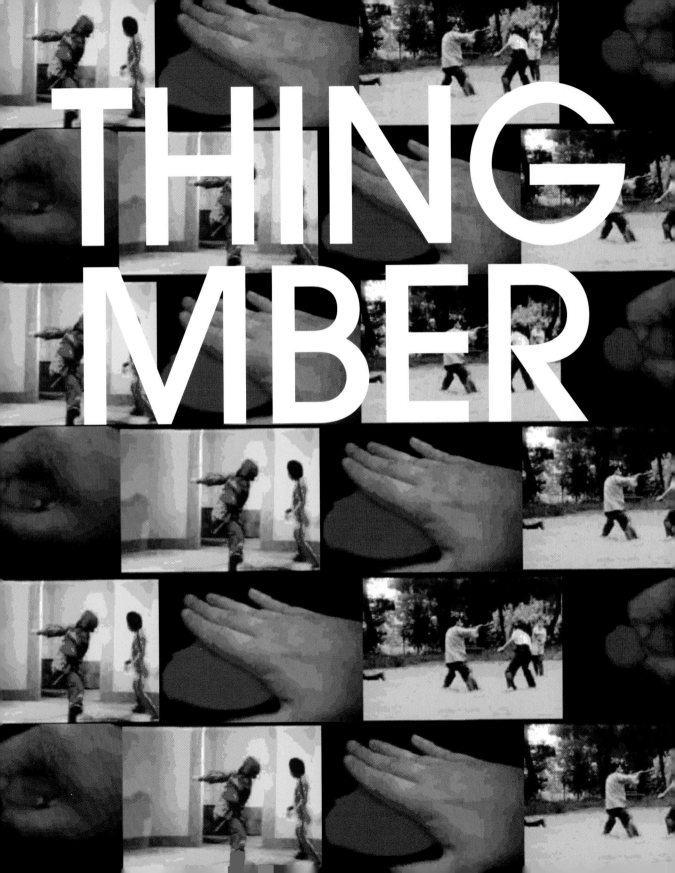

Helpful Sites

See for yourself how Play-Doh
can be used as a control device:

www.brendandawes.com/sketches/
play-doh/

Maker of the Max/MSP software
used to make the Play-Doh concept:

www.cycling74.com

Official site of Play-Doh:

www.hasbro.com/playdoh/

It's true that Play-Doh is not something you usually associate with computers. It has no electronic parts. No outputs. No inputs. But as the Greek philosopher Pythagoras would say, everything is number. If I could manipulate the Play-Doh and get that manipulation into a computer as a series of numbers, as it were—well, that opens up a world of possibilities.

Whenever I approach a problem like this, I break it down into smaller chunks because it's much easier to approach that way than as a whole. The digital bit that the Play-Doh controls could come later. First I needed to work out how to get information from the ball of Play-Doh into my Mac. I thought that the easiest way to do this would be via some kind of color tracking using a camera.

This is where the practice of experimentation and iteration really comes into its own. For about seven years, I've carried around a firewire hard disk on which I store hundreds of little experiments. I treat it like a digital storage box for folders of concepts and ideas, which I sometimes use straightaway and sometimes let sit for years until it is the right moment for them to spring forth into the world. Because it's portable, I can always have the firewire drive with me—at the office in Manchester, on a train traveling home, or in a hotel room in Chicago. It so happens that I had been playing around with tracking colors in one of these digital sketches. Now I had an idea to use that technique on.

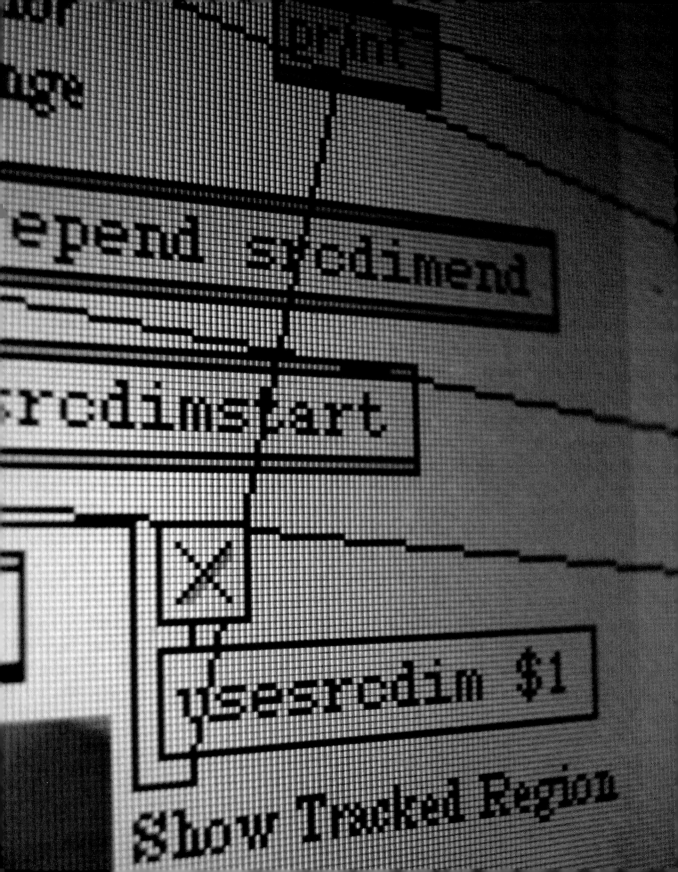

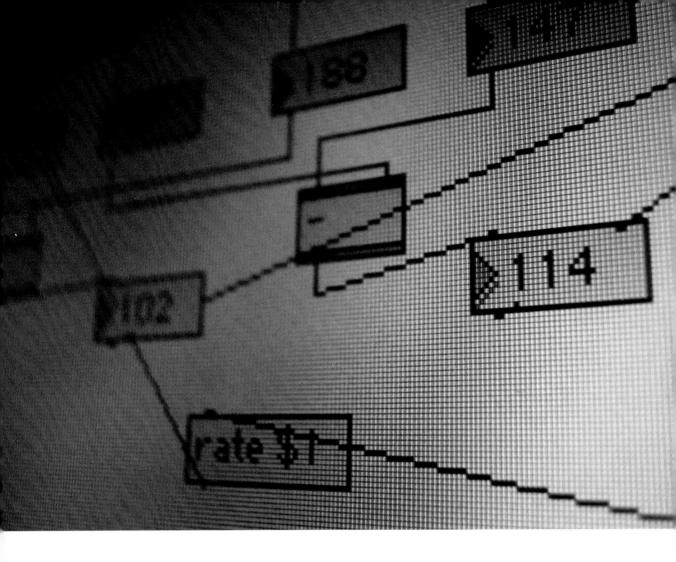

The software I used to develop the idea is Cycling74's Max/MSP. It is like no other programming environment that I've ever come across. Instead of typing in lines of code, you create objects on screen that you then "wire" together using patch cords. The first time I used Max, it took me about half an hour to make anything happen. But when I got a grip on the basics, I became obsessed with the power of what it could do, especially when it came to video processing using the Jitter extension. This was like a new toy to me. I had that child-like sense of wonder as I started to explore this strange yet power-ful new box of tricks.

Using my Apple iSight camera and Max/MSP with the Jitter extension, I created a program that could track the red color of the Play-Doh. Actually, it could track not only the color but also the size of the Play-Doh. At this point, all I wanted to do was show some numbers on the screen—the width and height of the Play-Doh, as well as its position in the x and y axis. Once I had those numbers coming in, the rest was up to me. How I was going to twist those numbers to have them control things was going to be interesting.

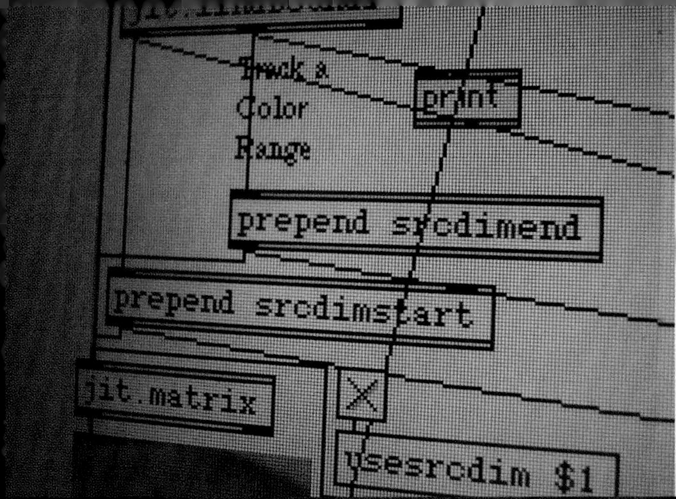

Track a
Color
Range

`print`

`prepend srcdimend`

`prepend srcdimstart`

`jit.matrix`

`usesrcdim $1`

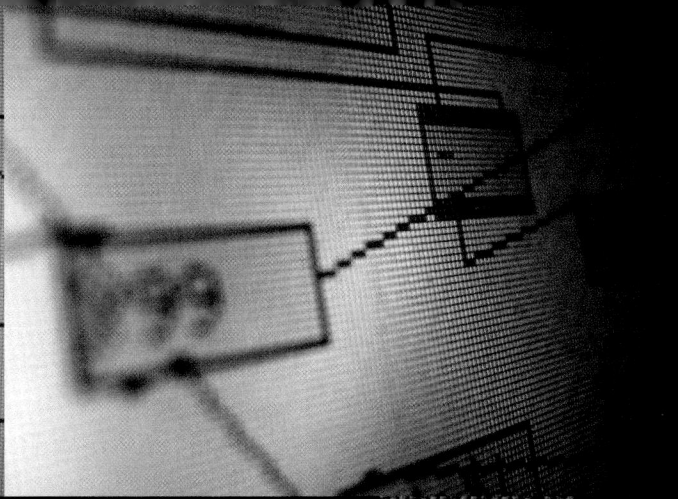

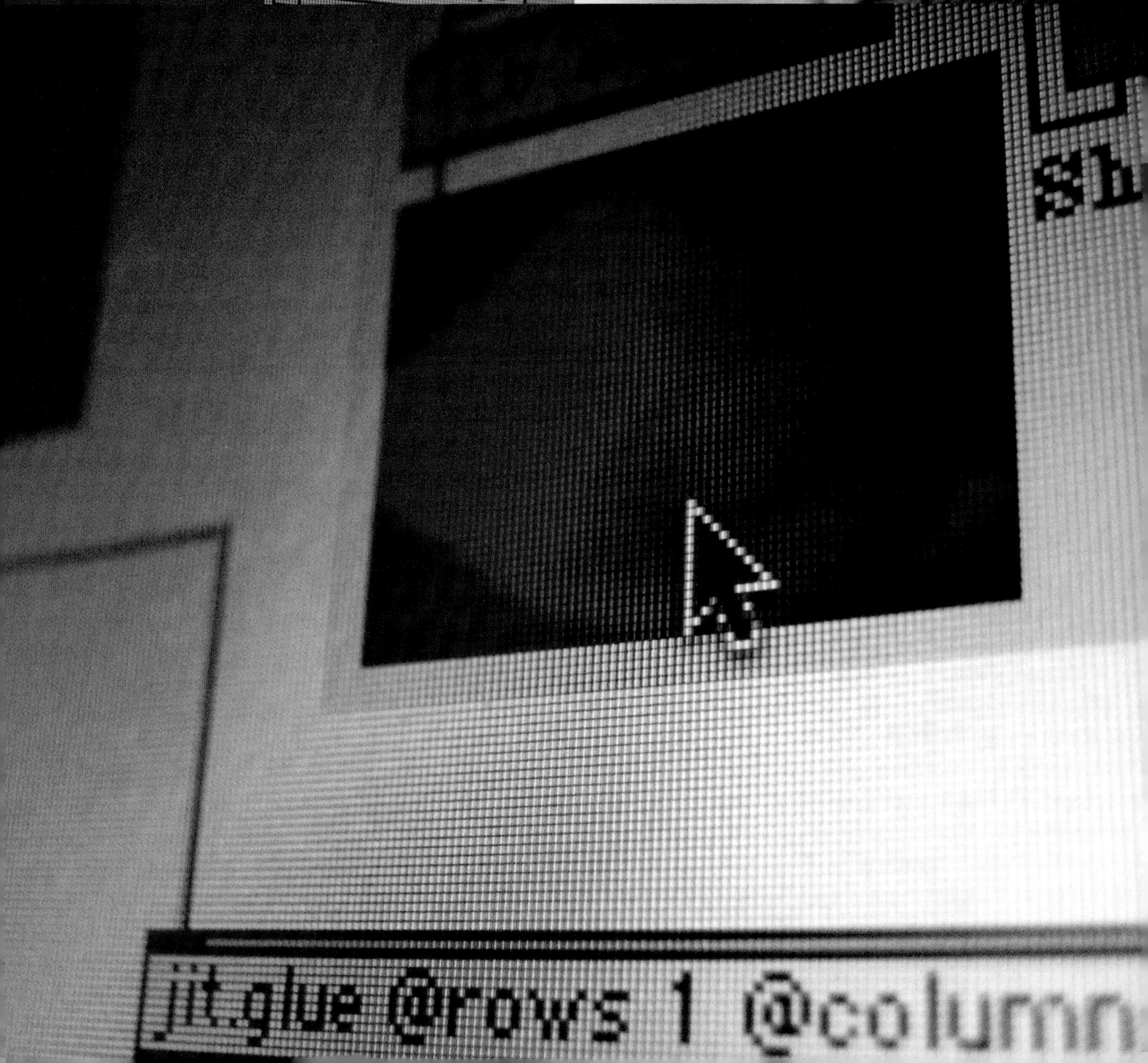

`jit.glue @rows 1 @column`

First off I made a very basic musical instrument simply by mapping numbers across a piano keyboard.

As you moved the Play-Doh across the screen, the software played notes from a piano, which sounded from the computer speakers. High notes when the Play-Doh moved to the top, low notes at the bottom. No wires. No touching a scary computer. Just rolling a ball of Play-Doh made notes appear as if by magic.

But this still didn't do it for me. It didn't really capture the unique qualities of a ball of Play-Doh—the fact that you can stretch it and squeeze it and alter its shape. It could just as well have been a red rubber ball. This is what iteration is all about: taking one idea and tweaking it into something else, and then doing it again and again and again. The problem is knowing when to stop!

I wasn't ready to stop. What about video? What about if I squashed the Play-Doh, spreading it larger on the screen to make a video play faster, then taking some away to make it go slower? Yeah, that would be cool. The only problem was that I had this idea the day before my session!

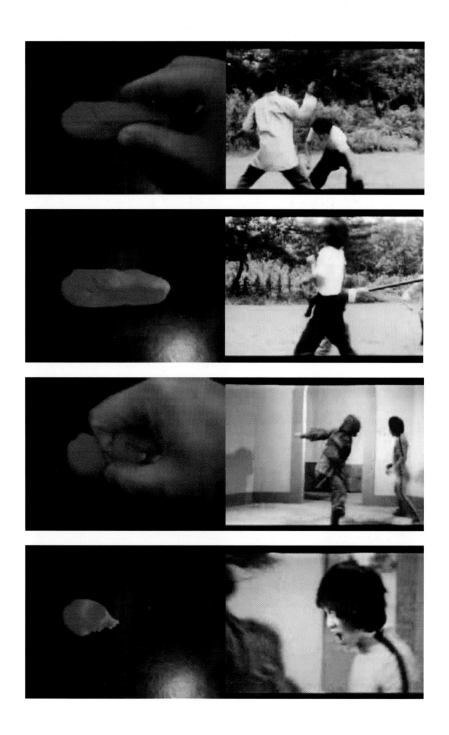

So that night I put the thing together in my hotel room. There was no time to think too much—I just had to get on and make it. I already knew I could get the width and height of the Play-Doh. Multiplied together, they equal the area, and the area would be another number to play with. I also had a sketch of how to control the speed of video in Max that had been sitting in my "storage box." I knew one day it would come in handy. By piecing together the calculation of the area of the Play-Doh and the video speed control, maybe I could get this idea to work.

And I did. It worked as if the Play-Doh was directly linked to the playing of the video, yet there didn't seemed to be any physical connection. It was just a ball of clay.

After showing this in my session, someone in the audience told me, "I couldn't believe what I was see-ing. It was like magic." That's one of the best things anyone has ever said to me about my work.

Yet someone else said, "It was cool and all that, but I can't see any application for it." Really? Just stop and think for a moment. Think about this from a child's point of view. Here's a ball of everyday Play-Doh, yet play with it and it does something extra magical. What about a specially made table with a camera inside that makes sounds and music when someone plays with balls of clay on its surface? Maybe you could make a music sequencer from different colored bits of Play-Doh or a simple movie mash-up machine by moving bits of it around.

It's interesting that I did not stop once to think about whether my original idea was even possible technically. I didn't care about that. I just thought, Here's a material that is incredibly tactile, that every-one is familiar with. Maybe it could be used as an interface. There was no "sensible" person in my ear saying that it couldn't be done. I think the possibili-ties for applying it are endless, especially in the area of learning tools for children. And yet even if there were no practical application for this idea, it altered my perception of what a human/machine interface can be.

space invaders

retro flash drive™

pace invaders

CX-2632

1-16   ONE PLAYER
17-112 TWO PLAYERS
128   MEGABYTES

*Trademark of Taito America Corp. 1980
Program contents © 1980 ATARI, INC.

Use with Joystick Controllers

∧ ATARI®

5

Recycling the Past

These days we live in a world where we're constantly being told to up-grade and update. It's the nature of a consumption-based culture that we habitually throw things away rather than find new ways to use them. So we end up being surrounded by lots of dead things. Bits of hardware that we'll never use again gather dust on our shelves like discarded toys in a child's nursery—sad, lonely, unloved, and unusable. But it doesn't have to be this way. Something that we once loved can actually be brought back to life and mutated into a different useful, fun object with a full future ahead.

ATARI
T.V.
GAME

The most popular T.V. Game on the market with a range of over 40 cartridges including SPACE INVADERS with over 112 games on one cartridge. **£95**.45 inc. VAT

Amongst all the bits of "presumed dead" hardware that I have at home is an old Atari video game system. Back in the '70s, the Atari 2600 was one of the first computer systems I owned, and I would while away hours and hours playing Space Invaders, Asteroids, and other such games on the TV in our front room. In many ways, playing with this humble game system was my first relationship with anything digital. This was an object that meant something to me. Yet there it sat without any prospects for the future.

One day I took a good look at some of the other stuff around me that's still in use. Call me a sentimental old romantic, but I don't think fondly of my much-needed USB hub—it would be a bit weird, for one thing. Surely, I thought, something that I use every day *should* have a bit more of an emotional attachment to it. Wait a minute...What if I took some bits of my old Atari system and remade them into actual useful objects? Objects that once again had "the capacity to be loved."

First up was that damned USB hub. I was constantly frustrated by having to grab my USB hub and fiddle around with the back of it to plug in my card reader so I could pull down my latest pictures from the memory card. So I took the nostalgic but outdated Atari joystick and the efficient but ugly-as-sin mini-portable USB hub, and fused the two together to create a new, retro-style USB hub. Now I can plug my stuff into something that means more to me than a nondescript piece of technology.

What else could I harvest from the Atari VCS and make use of? Hmm. Those cartridges are kind of cool looking. They were more or less the precursor to the memory stick. Hang on—did someone say *memory stick*?

Memory sticks, flash drives—whatever you want to call them—are undeniably remarkable. It still amazes me that I can carry 1GB of storage space in my pocket. Yet often I think that we are losing something with all this miniaturization of technology.

If you compare a storage device that can hold 256MB with a 1GB version, they look exactly the same. On the face of it, one is no bigger than the other. But people like how things feel, and sometimes we want to feel how big or small something is. Remember when you held a 12-inch record? It really felt like you were holding a lot of music, unlike a modern little CD. And my new Nikon camera feels solid in my hands. Before buying it, I read a lot of reviews that talked about how good it felt to hold. So now I wanted something that actually felt like it was holding my important stuff.

So I hacked up an old Atari 2600
cartridge and mutated it with
a USB drive. Atari cartridge, say
"hello" to USB drive. Now I have
an object that has the useful-
ness of those little memory
sticks that we know and love
but is also lovely looking—to
me, at least—and big enough to
take hold of. Of course, some
might think this is useless and
counterproductive—it certainly
seems to go against the whole
point of making data storage
devices smaller and lighter. But
for me, that faceless USB drive
now has a little bit of a story
attached to it. Somehow it is a
bit warmer and nicer to use.

How much do you have lying
around that could be repurposed, taken apart, and reused in
an original, interesting way?

6

All This Useless Beauty

There are a couple of projects I did a while back that are not really useful. In fact, they're probably a bit stupid. But for some reason, they fascinate people. Perhaps because we are living in a world that seems to celebrate the banal and mundane, we are especially captivated by the bizarre. Perhaps we simply need more stupid, fun things in life—things that do nothing but celebrate being utterly useless. Things that remind us of what it was like to play when we were kids. Or perhaps people are attracted to these projects because they mess with corporate culture and well-known icons—and that's got to be good.

Helpful Sites

Get all the info on the Google API:

www.google.com/apis

Developer info for Amazon's Web services:
www.amazon.com/gp/aws/landing.html

See for yourself what happens when Google is fused with McDonald's:

www.brendandawes.com/sketches/mcgoogle

View Amazon search results sideways:

www.brendandawes.com/sketches/flamazon

Many years ago, I kept the bottom of a McDonald's take-away bag. There was just something about it that I liked. I always thought those little symbols on the bottom of the bag were really well-designed pieces of iconography, and I thought that maybe I could use the bag bottom for something one day. So I cut it out, while my wife rolled her eyes, and put it to one side.

A few years later I was playing around with the Google API, just as you do. Basically, because it allows you to integrate Google search into your own projects, I could make a Flash version of Google if I wanted. But why would I want to do that? What's the point of replicating something that works well already? No, what I needed was something to help me create a little twist on the Google search engine—something crazy, something a bit strange, something like...the bottom of a McDonald's bag!

What if you could enter your search query on the bottom of the bag and get the results back as a series of burgers and fries? What? You heard me: Get your results back as a series of burgers and fries. So that's what I did. I made the world's first McGoogle. You want fries with that?

McGoogle

stupid

...ous anecdotes of
...ers creatively misusing
computers.

Heady with the accomplishment of mutating the world's most famous fast-food company with the world's most ubiquitous search engine, I turned my attention to seeing what other Web services could fuel some madcap data remixing.

Ah, Amazon has an API, just ripe for the mashing. Let's make a little Amazon search front end that looks as if it were in a '70s Swedish sauna. Hmmm, yeah, nice bits of pine. Then when we get the results back, let's turn everything on its side—after all, horizontal text is so last year! So there we have Flamazon—so much nicer than its stodgy cousin.

OK, I know: On the face of it, these projects are completely ridiculous. But then again, so what? Why should data always be presented in such a conser-vative manner? It's as if we're so awed by all that information that we feel we have to respect it in some way. Well I say: To hell with that. Get out there, have some fun, and start breaking things up!

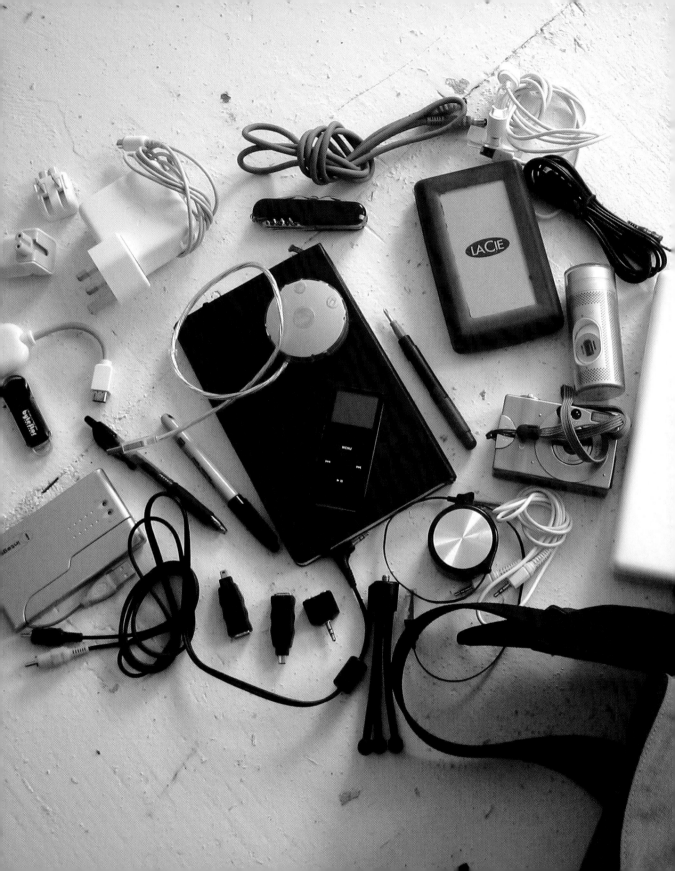

7

Anything Can Happen in the Next Half-Hour

Many people ask me how I create what seems like a large body of work on a seemingly constant basis. Is it because I never sleep? Or perhaps I have some kind of time machine that gives me working hours other people don't have?

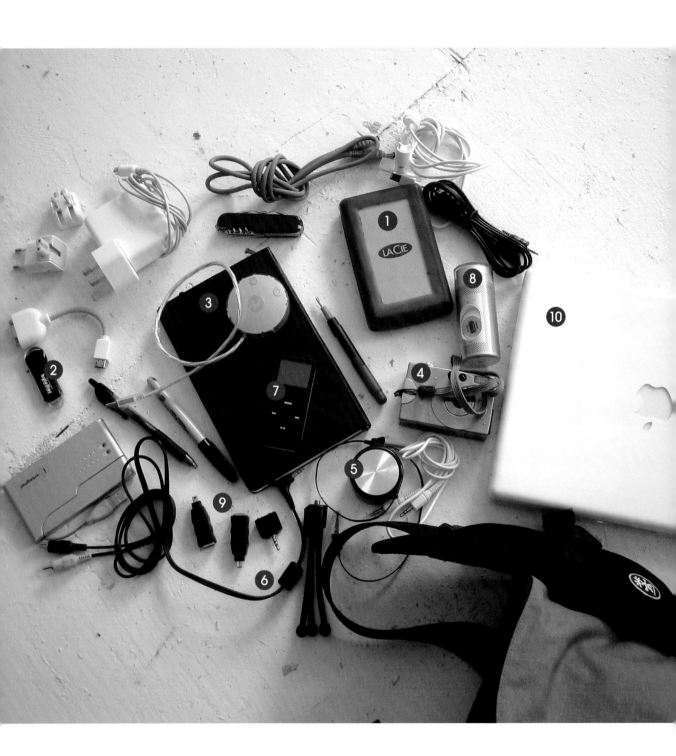

While I do like to make things constantly, I also like to work smarter, not necessarily harder. That's why I always have with me many of the "tools" I need to make stuff, no matter where I am. Creating on the fly, so to speak, also allows me to work "in the moment" and capitalize fully on the situation I'm in, rather than jotting down an idea and reconstructing the situation in my mind later. For example, when I was simply waiting in Los Angeles airport, I noticed the patterns of people passing me as they ran for their planes. With my "tools" handy, I was able to create a visual interpretation of that pattern. I discuss how I did this in the chapter "Waiting for Departure."

I've always got my 10-Gig FireWire drive (1) and a USB memory key (2), which has a little TiddlyWiki application, WikiOnAStick, so I can jot down anything that springs to mind. It also contains a folder with installers for my most used applications, in case I'm at a conference and my hard drive goes down or I need to reinstall anything. There's the essential notebook (3)—still the best "laptop" there is—and my digital camera (4) for taking quick snaps. Then I've got a few handy cables such as a spoolable

Ethernet wire (5); various audio cables (6) for connecting my iPod (7) so I can use the audio to drive various sound-driven graphic pieces; and the all-important Apple iSight camera (8), which is great for doing webcam, motion-detection stuff like the project in the "Play-Doh as Interface" chapter. I also carry various connectors/adapters (9) and converters to try to anticipate various technical situations that might require them.

Of course, I also have my 12-inch iBook (10). I went for the smallest iBook I could get because if you've ever tried opening a big laptop while sitting in Coach on an airplane, you know it's pretty impossible.

Armed with all this gear, I can create all sorts of digital work, no matter where in the world I am—providing there's at least some kind of power source!

8
Waiting for Departure

Whilst sitting at the departure gate at LAX waiting for my plane home from Los Angeles, I started to notice how the people rushing by seemed to come in patterns or waves. Maybe I could make something that would show these frequency patterns, I thought.

The people rushing by were essentially a creative input source. It didn't matter to me that the source was analog and not digital; it's all just numbers that can be put into a digital device.

I'm always fascinated by the idea of taking information like this and creating visuals from what I see. The people rushing by were essentially a creative input source. It didn't matter to me that the source was analog and not digital; it's all just numbers that can be put into a digital device, like my iBook.

So armed with my iBook and my iSight camera, a few minutes later I made a real-time graph generator using the Processing application. Essentially what's happening here is that the code compares the latest frame from the video camera to the last one and then sees how many pixels have changed. This is pretty much the basis of most motion-capture techniques.

Essentially what's happening here is that the code compares the latest frame from the video camera to the last one and then sees how many pixels have changed.

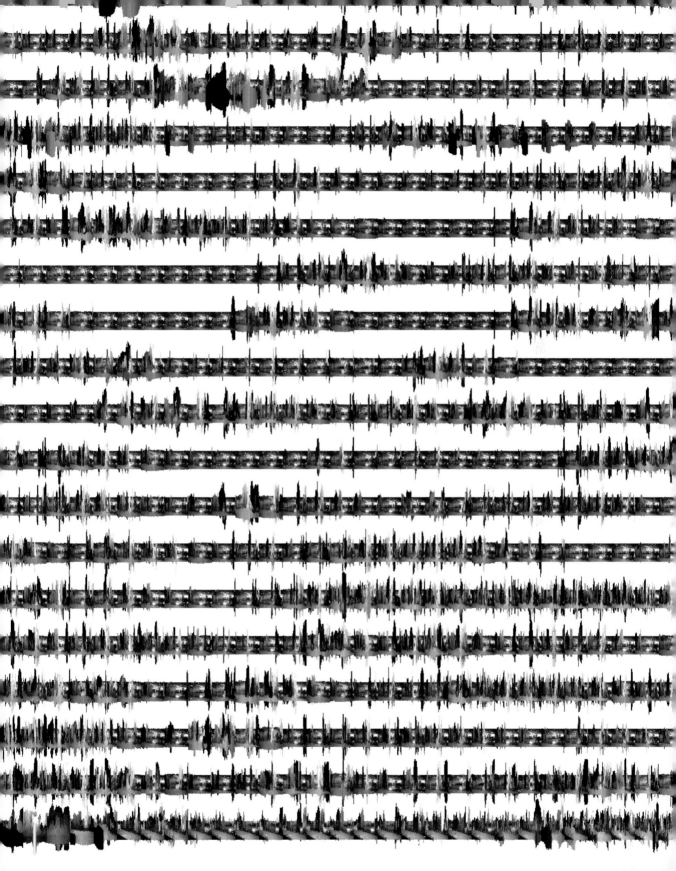

Notice how the graph gets "busier" the more activity there was passing me. You can start to see more of the scene at the times when there was more activity too. Why is it only 20 minutes long? Because I had to catch my plane!

Helpful Site

See an open source Java-based software for visual coders:

www.processing.org

9

Nightmare at 30,000 Feet

Traveling to speak at conferences around the world, I get to see many new places and meet some great people. But my professional travels are not always about what happens at the final destination. Along the way, I often see and experience many interactions between people and their environment that end up being part of what I take back to work with me. These interactions can only be experienced firsthand. They can't be imagined whilst at your desk; you need to bump into them for them to leave a mark on you.

Once, on a flight to San Francisco, I sat next to a couple who were returning from a six-week tour of the Middle East. Since it was a long flight, all the seats had in-flight entertainment built into the back of the headrest for the person in the seat behind. You could choose from a myriad of channels simply by touching the screen and using the in-screen interface. Now I'm sure this system had been tested quite thoroughly in expensive user-testing labs. But obviously it hadn't been tested on the guy who was sitting next to me, a guy we'll call "Buck."

DO NOT WALK IN

Buck started to press the screen in front of him repeatedly, trying to get to the channel he wanted to watch. Even though the system was "on," the movies had not yet started to play. But as far as Buck was concerned, the system wasn't working correctly. So he did what came naturally to him: He started hammering the screen with his big finger, attempting to prod the system into life through brute force. It reminded me of when you're in a hurry in a lift, so you press the button for your floor a zillion times. It doesn't help you get to where you're going any quicker, but it makes you feel better.

Now there's nothing wrong with prodding a machine occasionally; I do it myself all the time. But the problem here was that the "machine" was attached to a human—the person unlucky enough to be in the seat in front of Buck. Bash, bash, bash. That person's head was being pummeled from behind as Buck desperately tried to find a channel that actually worked. It was the domino effect: Buck's bad interface with the touch screen was now creating a bad flight experience for the person in front of him, and it wasn't very pleasant for me either. Eventually the passenger had enough of being a human remote control and turned around to "ask" Buck to stop punching his head. If only the flight experience was designed to be as calm and placid for passengers inside the airplane as the scenery was outside the window!

Buck started to press the screen in front of him repeatedly, trying to get to the channel he wanted to watch. Even though the system was "on," the movies had not yet started to play. But as far as Buck was concerned, the system wasn't working correctly.

"IS THIS THE VOLUME CONTROL?"

Once the movies did start, Buck was a lot happier. But it wasn't loud enough for him, so he looked around for the volume control. He completely missed the overlaid volume buttons on the plastic of the touch screen. Eventually, after trying every other thing that looked as if it might turn up the volume, he turned to me and asked, "Is this the volume control?" I saw that he had hold of the little round plastic coat hook just underneath the screen.

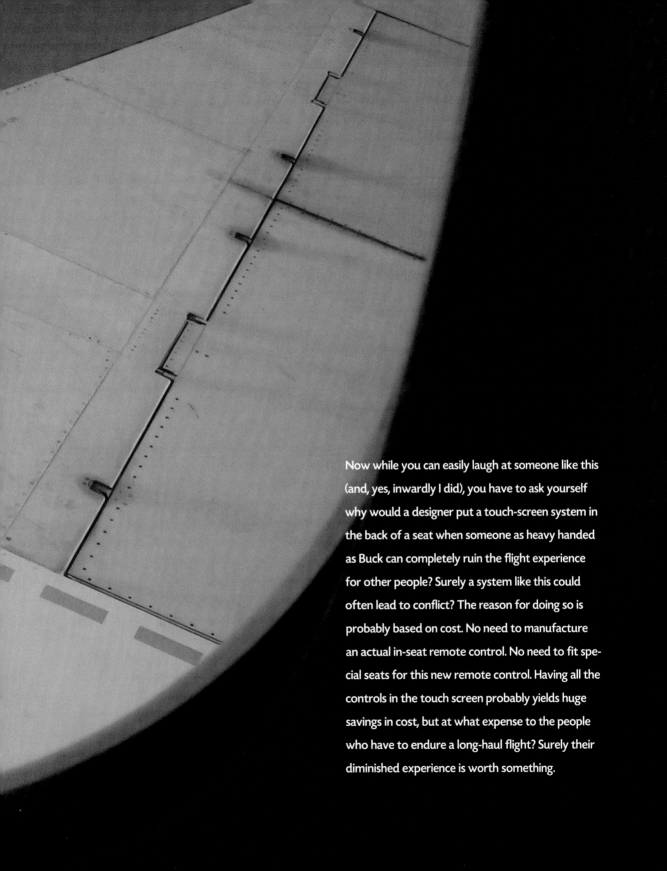

Now while you can easily laugh at someone like this (and, yes, inwardly I did), you have to ask yourself why would a designer put a touch-screen system in the back of a seat when someone as heavy handed as Buck can completely ruin the flight experience for other people? Surely a system like this could often lead to conflict? The reason for doing so is probably based on cost. No need to manufacture an actual in-seat remote control. No need to fit special seats for this new remote control. Having all the controls in the touch screen probably yields huge savings in cost, but at what expense to the people who have to endure a long-haul flight? Surely their diminished experience is worth something.

Having all the controls in the touch screen probably yields huge savings in cost, but at what expense to the people who have to endure a long-haul flight? Surely their diminished experience is worth something.

The volume-control conundrum is interesting for another reason. The problem with many touch-screen systems is their lack of physical interaction and visual feedback. Buck tried many options until in desperation he grabbed the thing that actually looked like a volume control. If you're not going to make your interface intuitive, at least provide some instructions that make it clear to people how to use it.

Booksale 317
393-397 Lord Street
Southport
Merseyside
PR9 0AG

01704 547383

DATE: 21/04/2006 TIME: 15:06
TILL: 0507   NO: 50733498
CASHIER: JOANNE

DESCRIPTION	£
Concise French Dicti	1.00 C
Concise Spanish Dict	1.00 C

2 PC. TOTAL	£2.00
CASH	£2.00

VAT C 0.00% (£2.00): £0.00

Selected Paperbacks
£1.99 Each
3 For £5

10

Strangers on a Train

As I live 40 miles away from Manchester and the magneticNorth studio, I travel by train every day. While it's a pain being tied to a commute time and at the mercy of the incredibly bad British transport system, the train is great for doing a lot of thinking and for observing the behavior of fellow passengers. By putting myself in a situation where lots of interaction takes place between strangers and acquaintances, I see unexpected things happen all the time—things that open my mind up to new ways of thinking. By far the nicest occurred out of the blue the evening before I wrote this piece.

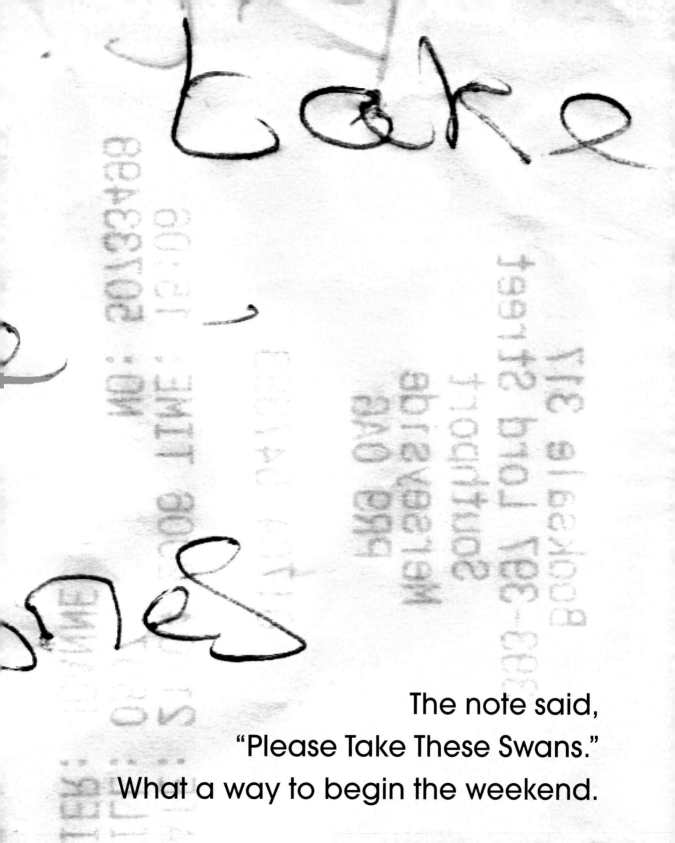

The note said,
"Please Take These Swans."
What a way to begin the weekend.

There I am, sitting on the train, scheduled to arrive home at around eight—a decent enough time compared to the rest of the week, when I'd been getting in close to midnight. It's Friday, so the week has taken its toll, and I'm drifting off to sleep now and again. As usual the train is packed, the seats across from me all occupied with passengers minding their own business, most of them reading the free newspaper you get rammed into your hand at the train station as you head home.

I drift into a cat's nap. When I come to, about ten minutes later, I notice something on the seat where a passenger was sitting just minutes before. The passenger has disappeared, leaving behind a piece of paper, a till receipt, with "P.T.O." written on it.

It's a message. Is it for me? Who left it? There is no way I can ignore the paper—I must see why I am being asked to *please turn over*.

I grab the paper and flip it over. There, in uncertain English, it says on the other side, "Please take these swans," with an arrow pointing down.

Swans? What swans?

I look back to the seat and realize that the bits of paper I thought were just rubbish are actually origami swans! And they are for me. What a way to start the weekend—receiving origami swans from a mysterious stranger.

So why am I even telling you this story? It's a nice little anecdote, but surely this has nothing to do with design?

Well, actually it does. What really struck me about this incident was the way the message was written. The author could have simply jotted down, "Take these swans," on the front of the paper, so I would see it straightaway. Instead, intentionally or not, the person added an extra layer of intrigue with the message "P.T.O." It was like coming upon a slightly open door to a room you've always wanted to see—impossible not to be drawn into peeking at what may or may not lie on the other side. Here on a humdrum journey from Manchester, a train ride I take every night, was a brilliant lesson in suspense and drama. All it took was some words on an old receipt, a pen, and a bit of imagination.

11

Spiral Notebook

The great Charles Eames, half of the legendary California design house Eames Studio, once commented that far more important than innovation is the process of iteration. After all, while an automobile with the driver's seat facing backward could be called innovative, would it actually advance the design of the motorcar? In fact, it would do the exact opposite. But in design, the craft of iteration—for I believe it is a craft—can lead to constant improvement via experimentation and abstraction.

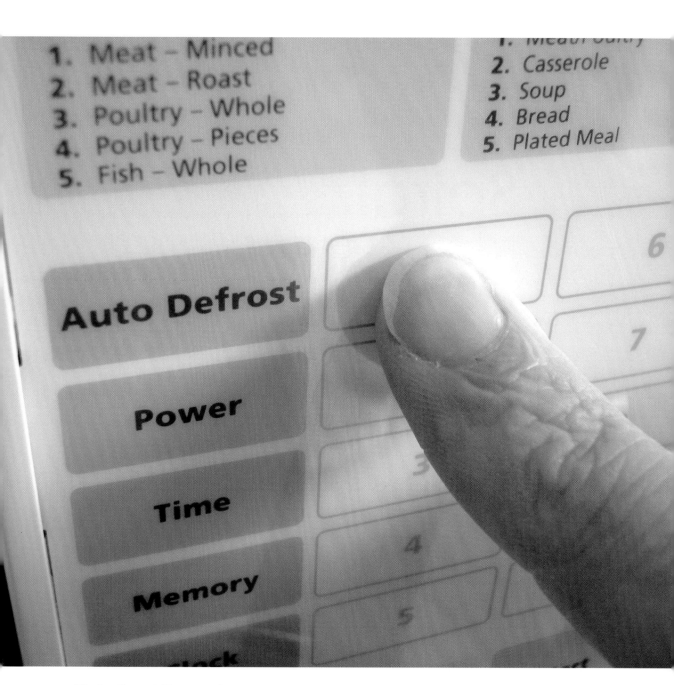

1. Meat – Minced
2. Meat – Roast
3. Poultry – Whole
4. Poultry – Pieces
5. Fish – Whole

1. Meat/Poultry
2. Casserole
3. Soup
4. Bread
5. Plated Meal

Auto Defrost

Power

Time

Memory

6

7

Altering the variables on a microwave oven.

As I mention elsewhere in this book, I always carry with me a ten-gig firewire hard drive—full of source files, bits of code, photos, and notes—that works with my iBook as a kind of digital sketchbook. This is full of many iterations—ideas that start out as one thing and lead to other, usually more interesting things. Within one idea folder, I may have 50-plus files that each build on the one before it. These are all a chain of variations. Oftentimes there may be just one line of code or one variable that differs from one file to the next. But that single variable, that one small change, could lead to another way of thinking and a better solution to a problem.

When I mention the word "variable," probably the first thing you think of is algebra or some kind of programming language. Variables are at the heart of every programming language, but they're also at the heart of *everything* in life. We process / make / use variables every second of our lives—it's just that we don't think of them in that way.

Right now your eyes are processing a constantly changing "sight" variable. Your eyes are putting all the visual information on the page and in your peripheral vision into a "sight box," which your brain then processes. When you punch in the cooking time on a microwave oven, you're punching in variables such as seconds and minutes. You're altering variables, which then affects the output of the process—in this case how well nuked, or cooked, the food will be. It's effectively an iteration. Not cooked enough? No problem; alter your variables to suit and see what comes out the other end. It's experimentation, and you're using creative programming principles to do it!

Variables are at the heart of every programming language, but they're also at the heart of *everything* in life. We process / make / use variables every second of our lives—it's just that we don't think of them in that way.

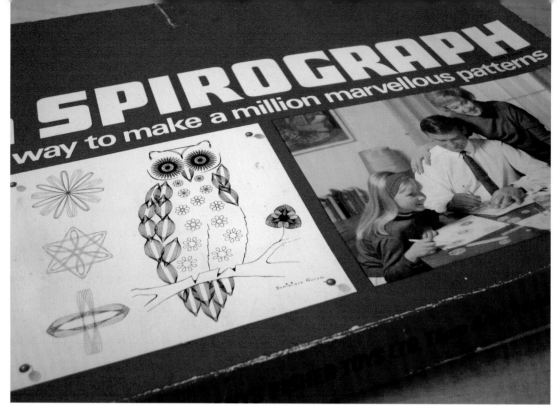

The Spirograph is all about playing with variables.

The very old Spirograph toy in the photo really demonstrates well the process of altering variables simply to see what happens.

The instructions for "using a series of wheels" sets up a whole load of variables: the pin ring number, which hole to put the pen into, and which wheel to use. Altering just one of these variables—the wheel number, for example—will create a different pattern. In this case, all we're doing is altering some numbers to see how that affects the end result. The process of altering a number, no matter how small an alteration, and continuing to iterate can often lead to startling differences in the eventual output. Let's look at an example.

Altering the size of the wheel—just one variable—produces a different result.

Helpful Sites

Download the Processing application:

http://www.processing.org/

A spiral used to display photos:

http://www.brendandawes.com/sketches/flickrtimetunnel

A magneticNorth site that uses the dynamic navigation system:

http://www.newislington.co.uk

Read more about Lissajous curves:

http://en.wikipedia.org/wiki/Lissajous

I've always been fascinated by the opening titles for Alfred Hitchcock's *Vertigo*. Graphic designer and film title genius Saul Bass worked with John Whitney on the opening sequence to create beautiful spiral shapes that appear out of the darkness. John Whitney was a computer graphics pioneer who applied the knowledge he had gained creating missile guidance systems for Douglas Aircraft to the field of motion graphics—an iteration of his own skills. After all, if he could create and map trajectories for missiles, he could use the same principles to control motion camera rigs and the like.

After doing some research on how Whitney created those beautiful spiral shapes, I found that the algorithms he used were called Lissajous waves, named for Jules Antoine Lissajous, a 19th century mathematician who was fascinated by waves and developed a way to visualize them. After some hunting around, I managed to find the basic algorithm for generating Lissajous waves, which I then worked into a little program in Processing, a free open source programming environment (which can easily be ported into Flash).

```
float xMid;
float yMid;
float x;
float y;
float lastX;
float lastY;
float r = 255;
float g = 255;
float b = 255;
void setup() {
 size (500,500);
 xMid = width/2;
 yMid = height/2;
 background(0);
 stroke(255);
 smooth();
 makeSpiral();
}
void loop() {
 background(0);
 makeSpiral();
}
void makeSpiral() {
 for (int c=0; c < 1132; c++) {
  stroke(r,g,b,30);
  x = xMid + 150*sin(c/((mouseX/10.0)/5.0));
  y = yMid + 150*cos(c/((mouseY/10.0)/5.0));
  if (c==0) {
   line(x,y, x,y);
  } else {
   line(lastX,lastY, x,y);
  }
  lastX = x;
  lastY = y;
 }
}
void mousePressed() {
 saveFrame();
}
```

This used the X and Y position of the mouse as a user-controlled variable to generate Lissajous wave patterns. The depth and breadth of patterns are incredible when you consider the small amount of code needed to generate these images, all because of the power of the variable—in this case an X and a Y.

But then I wanted to see the relationship between one pattern and another. What was the difference between an X value of 1 and, say, an X value of 5? How much does it alter the resulting pattern? So I created another iteration of the above code, but this time, after displaying a pattern, the X value was increased by 5 by the code itself. If the X value was more than the width of the stage, then X was set back to 0 and the Y value was increased by 5. And so on and so on. Here are the results from the first few patterns.

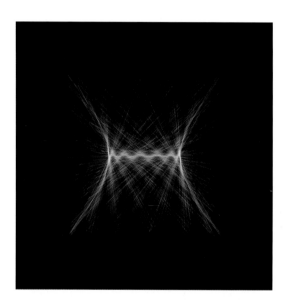

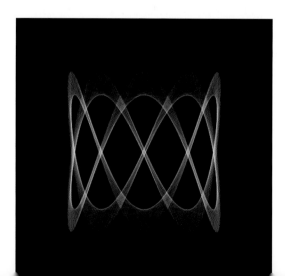

Same algorithm, different variables. Why didn't they teach me stuff like this in school?

Notice that each iteration of a pattern is pretty similar until *kapow*—you get a mutant form that is radically different. And yet what makes, say, the V-shaped pattern different from the ones before and after it is simply a tiny variation in one or two variables. As the *Sesame Street* song "One of These Things (Is Not Like the Others)" says, tiny alterations can make a big difference. Such is the power of variables and iteration.

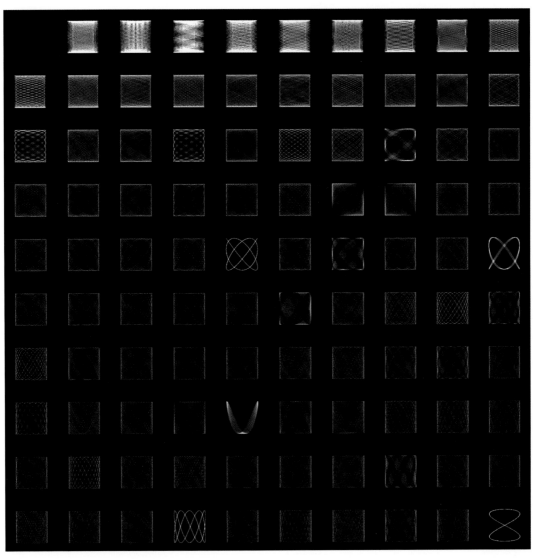

Small variations in Lissajous wave patterns. But wait—some are very different....

Photos from FlickrTimeTunnel displayed around a spiral.

But I still wasn't finished with the possibilities of what a simple spiral algorithm could do; more iteration was needed. Rather than thinking about creating patterns and graphic art, it struck me that a spiral places points around a center with an ever-growing diameter. I could use that principle to place objects in a spiral—photographs, perhaps—and make the spiral represent time, with the center being furthest away in time, as it were.

With this in mind, I created what I called the FlickrTimeTunnel, inspired by the use of a spiral. To enhance the sense of the passage of time, I added a bit of blur to some of the photographs, based on when they were taken (ahh, another variable), making them seem to disappear into the swirling currents of time.

What else could you build off the back of an algorithm like this? What about if you stop the diameter from increasing and plot nodes around a center point? You may have the beginnings of a scalable circular navigation system.

So that's a cool thing to do with photos, but what else could you build off the back of an algorithm like this? What about if you stop the diameter from increasing and plot nodes around a center point? You may have the beginnings of a scalable circular navigation system. A system like this could be advantageous when you don't know how many navigational points you may need because any number of points could be equally distributed around a center point. For example, it could be a dynamic navigation system that had to be flexible enough to cope with different amounts of navigation points but always look like they were placed around a center point by hand. After a few bits of trial and error, I had code in Flash that would create as many nodes around a center point as needed.

```
function createNodes() {
    var a:Number = 0;
    var d:Number = 100; // distance from center
    var x:Number = (Stage.width/2);
    var y:Number = (Stage.height/2);
    var amount:Number = 5;
    var inc:Number = (Math.PI*2)/amount;
    for (c=0; c<amount; c++) {
        a += inc;
        var o:MovieClip = attachMovie("node", "node"+c, c,{_x:
x+Math.sin(a)*d,_y:y+Math.cos(a)*d});
    }
}
createNodes();
```

It gave me this.

Nodes placed dynamically around a center point.

Then simply by the process of iteration, I replaced the number that I specified in the amount variable with the number of items that are placed in a nodes array, like so:

```
nodes = new Array("what","where","how","why","if","maybe");
function createNodes() {
    // creates circular node based nav
    var a:Number = 0;
    var d:Number = 100; // distance from center
    var x:Number = (Stage.width/2);
    var y:Number = (Stage.height/2);
    var amount:Number = nodes.length; // amount of nodes
    var inc:Number = (Math.PI*2)/amount;
    for (c=0; c<amount; c++) {
        a += inc;
        var o:MovieClip = attachMovie("node", "node"+c, c,{_x:
x+Math.sin(a)*d,_y:y+Math.cos(a)*d});
        if (o._x > x) {
        o.gotoAndStop("showright");
        } else {
        o.gotoAndStop("showleft");
        }
        o.item.text = nodes[c];
    }
}
createNodes();
```

how

why   where

if   what

Now we start to see how these "nodes"
maybe   are turned into a navigation device.

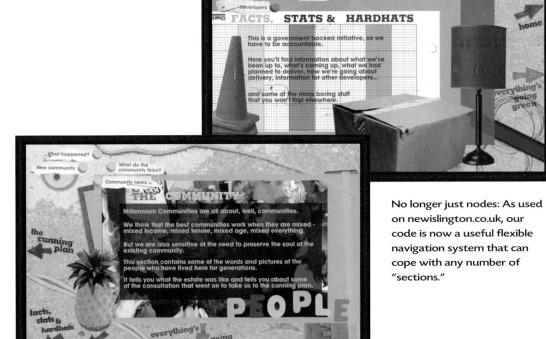

No longer just nodes: As used on newislington.co.uk, our code is now a useful flexible navigation system that can cope with any number of "sections."

By the time I finished my exploration of spiral algorithms (for this journey at least), I'd gone from making pretty patterns to creating a visual way to display photos chronologically to formulating ideas for scalable navigation systems that are customizable by altering simple variables such as the size of the circle to the number of nodes in the navigation.

Iterating design through the use of variables is a core concept of the work I do. What's key is thinking in an abstract way. It may not be an obvious leap from Lissajous waves and spirals to a device to create a dynamic navigation system, but that's the point of iteration and exploration—to evolve an idea from simple origins to a place you never thought of before.

Revolutionaries: John Whitney

Revolutionaries: John Whitney is recognized as one of the founders of computer graphics. In the 1950s, he made incredible analog machines that could create stunning math-based art, which led to him to working with Saul Bass on the title sequence for Alfred Hitchcock's Vertigo. What really appeals to me about John Whitney, though, is that he worked mapping out missile guidance systems for Douglas Aircraft when he realized that the very machines that directed missiles to their targets could be used to create something beautiful. Find out more at http://www.siggraph.org/artdesign/profile/whitney/early.html.

12

The Power of Silence

One of my all-time movie heroes is Steve McQueen. I think the first thing I ever saw him in was *The Great Escape*. To me McQueen exuded exactly what it meant to be a Hollywood movie star. Yes, he could act, but he also had a terse magnetism that many more animated actors lacked. I still look to him to inspire my work as a designer.

Steve McQueen was an incredibly subtle actor. Just watch the scene where he first appears with Yul Brynner in the classic western *The Magnificent Seven*, and you'll see what I mean. Brynner had the lead, with more lines than anyone else in the film. Yet McQueen steals the scene from under Brynner's nose—and he does so without words. He does it by simply fiddling with his cowboy hat! The usually charismatic Brynner simply disappears into the background, and all you notice is the incredibly cool McQueen.

Steve McQueen seemed to possess a sixth sense of how to just do enough to communicate a character's personality—or even an entire back-story. This was true minimalism at work: the power of subtlety and silence.

McQueen seemed to possess a sixth sense of how to just do enough to communicate a character's personality—or even an entire back-story. When he received a script, he would strip out hundreds of words, and when he had done that, he'd do it again. Eventually the script was honed to just the essentials necessary to communicate the character or the plot. This was true minimalism at work: the power of subtlety and silence.

Now each time I approach a new design, each time I review a piece of work, I think back to Mr. McQueen and remove anything that isn't absolutely necessary to get the message across. Eventually the design becomes a whole lot purer because of this process.

For me, a beautiful example of how reduction can lead to stronger design is the iPal, from Tivoli Audio. The iPal is an AM/FM radio that doubles as a speaker for your personal stereo, MP3 player, and, of course, the ubiquitous iPod. I bought this more than 18 months ago, mainly so that when I'm on holiday or stuck in a hotel room, I can have music on without having to resort to using headphones. But what I really love about the iPal, compared to other speaker systems, is that it's rechargeable, so once it's charged, it doesn't need any connection to the mains for power.

What we're talking about in this chapter is reduction: What things have been taken away to add to the beauty of this product?

What we're talking about in this chapter, though, is reduction: What things have been *taken away* to add to the beauty of this product? Well, the first thing you notice is that it has only one speaker. Yep, that's right; it's mono. Though you need a few feet between each speaker to achieve true stereo separation, that would make a portable speaker system not very, well, portable. And this is one of the key benefits of the iPal. So the second speaker was removed because, quite frankly, it wasn't needed—the sound is still better than any micro two-speaker system, in my opinion. Then there are a few other details that deserve mention, such as the missing word "volume" with the volume control; instead, volume is indicated by a symbol that most people are familiar with. Also, on the marked-out frequencies around the tuning knob, the designers put just two markers on the knob itself—one points to FM and the other to AM. No need to mark AM or FM anywhere. It is just simplicity itself.

The bit that I absolutely love is the biggest thing that's missing. Notice how the "input" selector specifies AM, FM but no LINE input for your iPod. So how do you select the LINE input? Simple. You just plug it in around the back and the speaker switches to LINE input automatically. Beautiful. Want to listen to your iPod? Simply plug it in and you're done! There is no need to have a three-way switch, no need to switch to a specific mode. Plugging the plug into the back is the switch!

The iPal exudes simple, well thought-out design because it eliminates the noise of unnecessary elements and is stripped down to an essence that is both beautiful and completely intuitive to use. One day I hope to make something this good.

13

Jazz Inspiration

I listen to many types of music, but the genre I usually have on the stereo when I'm making stuff is jazz. I'm not talking Kenny G. I mean classic jazz from the likes of John Coltrane, Miles Davis, Oscar Peterson, and Thelonious Monk. To me, bebop-style jazz played live is about as pure as creativity gets. No time to chin-rub a particular note—just go with the flow and see where it takes you.

The letters of Thelonious Monk's name placed by sound-frequency information from the song "Monk's Dream."

What if I could create a series of sketches and experiments that are a visual interpretation of an entire track, a kind of sonic painting?

For me, the true standout in the world of jazz is Thelonious Monk. The first time I heard Monk's music, I thought, *What the hell is going on? This sounds awful.* Notes in places they shouldn't be, timing structures all over the place—all twisted and distorted like I'd never heard. But then, isn't that what I try to do with visual images? Isn't that what a lot of digital artists do—bend and shape bits of code, bits of data, into new forms, in the hope that something exciting will come of it? And the more I forced myself to listen to Monk and those like him, the more it struck me that they're all essentially hackers. But instead of hacking with computers to change code, they hacked with instruments to twist and reshape musical notes.

So then I asked myself: What if you could actually *see* those notes being played? What if I could create a series of sketches and experiments that are a visual interpretation of an entire track, a kind of sonic painting?

A snapshot from a typographic interpretation of John Coltrane's "Blue Train."

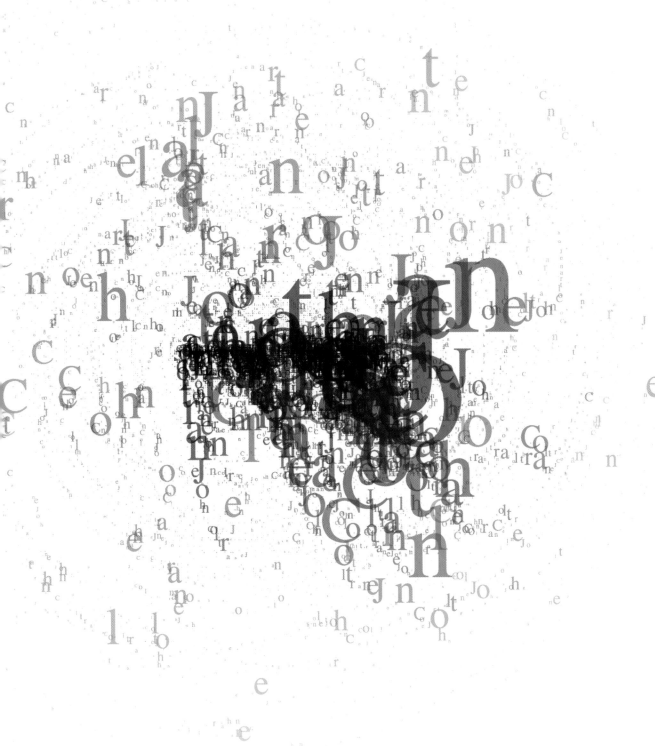

Helpful Sites

**Home of Amit Pitaru and his
Sonia sound library:**

http://sonia.pitaru.com/

Download the Processing application:

http://www.processing.org/

Now I'm not talking here about those cheesy iTunes screensaver things that react to sound. Though they're cute, they don't really communicate the music or the artist in any way, shape, or form. What I wanted to do was create some work that actually *looked* crafted, as if the musical notes created it as they were played.

Using the fabulous electronic sketchbook Processing, I started to put together some rough experiments. Now you might ask, "Why use Processing?" First, because Amit Pitaru—whom some of you may know from his early work with Flash—has written a great sound library that allows you to analyze sound input in real time. Second, Processing can save its output as PDFs, so I could load them into Photoshop and resize them for printing without losing any quality.

The basic algorithm I decided to use was based on mapping a spiral to the frequencies of the sound and then placing colored circles of varying opacity and size around that spiral, according to the frequency information. I've got to be honest with you: It's a total hacked-together piece of code, but you know what? It works!

Miles Davis' "Rocker" as seen through the basic algorithm.

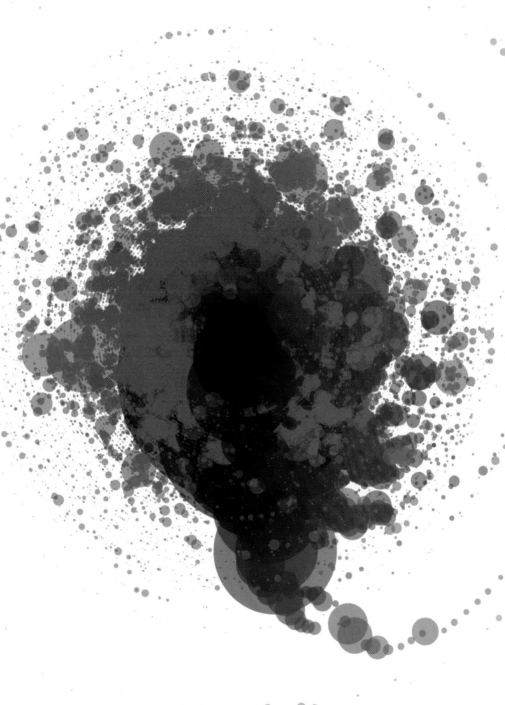

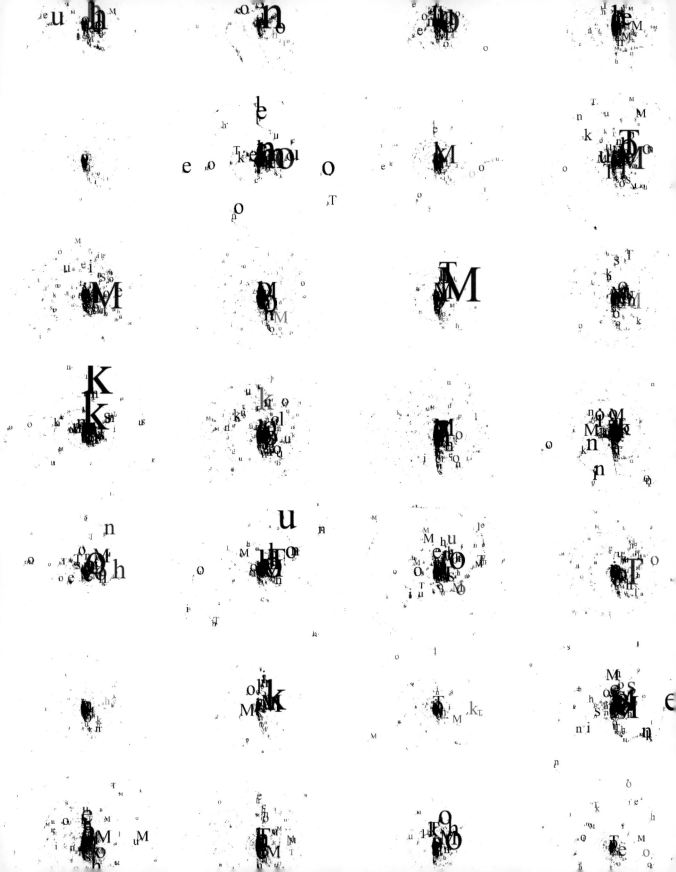

Basic Algorithm for Sonic Illustrations

```
import processing.pdf.*;

import pitaru.sonia_v2_9.*;

int xpos = 5;
float a = 0.0;
float inc = PI/0.3;
float[] spectrum;
float x,y,px,py;

void setup(){

  size(500,400);
  spectrum = new float[1024];
  Sonia.start(this);
  LiveInput.start(1024);
  rectMode(CENTER);
  ellipseMode(CENTER);
  colorMode(RGB, 256);
  smooth();
  background(255);

}


void draw() {

  getSpectrum();

}
```

```
void getSpectrum(){
  noStroke();
  spectrum = LiveInput.getSpectrum();
  float v = LiveInput.getLevel() * 10;
  for ( int i = 0; i < spectrum.length/4; i++){
    float r = (400.0/1000.0) * spectrum[i];
    float r1 = (400.0/1000.0) * spectrum[i+1];
    fill(i*5, xpos, 0,150);
    float w = (10.0/400.0) * r;
    ellipse((width/2)+sin(a)*xpos,
(height/2)+cos(a)*xpos,w,w);
    inc = PI/r1;
    a += inc;
    xpos += r/100.0;
  }
  a = 0.0;
  xpos = 1;

}

void mousePressed() {
  background(255);
}

void keyPressed() {
  exit();

}


public void stop(){

  Sonia.stop();
  super.stop();

}
}
```

A typographic sequence from Thelonious Monk's "Bemsha Swing."

Below: Röyksopp's "In Space."

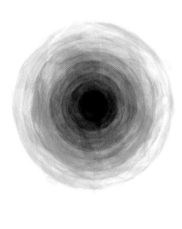

Above: Prince's "It's Gonna Be Lonely."
Top right: Radiohead's "Creep."
Bottom right: Rage Against the Machine's "Bullet in the Head."

Then it was just a case of iterating different approaches for different songs.

But why even bother doing this? Who actually needs it?

Well, with the advent of digital music downloads, we no longer really have anything as tangible as the album cover to provide a visual representation of the music within—and besides, people now buy individual tracks rather than whole albums. A graphic designer can't make a visual interpretation of every track, if for no other reason than it would be too costly.

A section from Miles Davis' "So What."

This is where something like this technique could come in. Perhaps in the future, the "album cover" creator will be an interactive designer or a pure programmer: a digital artist who creates coded interpretations of individual songs, created by some crazy program on the iTunes server that can dish up cool visual downloads for each track.

14

Close to You

One of the concepts I've exploited many times in projects is that of proximity—how close you are to things and the relationship that transpires as a result of that distance. The code for determining the distance between two points is pretty simple, but it can be used to solve many varied and complex design problems. For instance, you can use it to reveal more information as users get nearer to a certain point on the screen, or to make the volume increase as they creep up on an object, or to make a film speed up or slow down depending on how near they are to the center of the frame.

At magneticNorth, where I'm executive creative director, we used this idea in the Web site we designed for New Islington, an exciting housing redevelopment project in East Manchester, here in the U.K. All the way through the community redesign, the project's developers consulted the original residents about what it should include and what kind of place they wanted to live in—after all, this was and would continue to be their home. The developers also saw fit to make visual and audio records of what the residents thought about the area and the new development, which was fortunate for our part of the project.

Helpful Sites

See proximity design in action:

www.newislington.co.uk

(Go to "community" and then to "what happened," and select "residents' stories.")

Download some Flash source code that calculates proximities with the Drag Slide Fade 2.0 classes:

www.brendandawes.com/downloads

When we were scoping out ideas for the New Islington Web site, we knew we wanted to have these audio interviews on there, but simply listing a load of MP3s wouldn't communicate a sense of community or be very interesting. We wanted the site visitor's interaction with the recorded interviews to convey the feeling of community as much as the residents' actual words did.

So we used the proximity technique. We positioned little photos of each interviewee around a central picture frame, each linked to snippets of audio from their interviews. The volume of people's audio was determined by how close their pictures were to the frame. Now, as soon as you go to this part of the site, you jump into what seems like a lively conversation—many people chatting and discussing things. Want to hear what that person in the corner has to say? No problem, just drag her photo nearer to the center and move the others farther away. It's as if you are actually moving nearer to someone in a crowded room because you're interested in what she's saying.

esidents' storles

Main menu

's stories

WHAT HAPPENED ?

john
play full interview>

home

You jump into what seems like a lively conversation—many people chatting and discussing things. Want to hear what that person in the corner has to say? No problem, just drag her photo nearer to the center and move the others farther away.

Here is the basic code for calculating the distance between two points.
It's written in Flash but can easily be ported to other languages. What
you do with the number you get back is totally up to you.

```
var targetX:Number;
var targetY:Number;
var deltaX:Number;
var deltaY:Number;
var distance:Number;
this.onMouseMove = function() {
    // works out the distance of your mouse from the center of the screen
    targetX = Stage.width/2;
    targetY = Stage.height/2;
    deltaX = Math.round(_xmouse-targetX);
    deltaY = Math.round(_ymouse-targetY);
    // calculate the distance between the points
    distance = Math.round(Math.sqrt((deltaX*deltaX)+(deltaY*deltaY)));
    // do something with that number
    trace(distance);
}
```

39 #

euro 96
England

PT

BRENDON DAWES

DAILY STAR

TOURNAMENT

15

Don't Think

I've always been a big fan of instinct. And I think a lot of that comes from working as a photographer— specifically, the time I spent working part-time for my dad around 1996. My dad, John Dawes, has been a newspaper photographer all his life—it's all he's ever known. Most of that time, he's been a sports photographer, covering a lot of the world's major sporting events over the last four decades.

Shoot, choose, cut,

For a few years, I worked with my dad at many football (or, to you Americans, soccer) matches around the U.K. I was always amazed at how every picture on every job was important to him. It didn't matter that today's news would be "tomorrow's fish-and-chip paper." He always behaved as if his life depended on each frame. To me he was, and in many ways still is, the ultimate professional. His passion for his job meant he cared about every single image; "good enough" never came into it.

One of the key lessons I learned from my father is that you're only as good as your last job. You may have turned in some great photos last night, but that won't matter one jot when you submit your photos tonight. By his ethic, there is absolutely no room for complacency.

My job was to run around the football pitch at various times throughout the games, grab the rolls of film, develop them, scan them, and then send the newspaper a selection of images over the modem using the trusty Mac PowerBook. Of course, now this is all digital, with no film in site, but back then (and we're only talking a few years ago), you were mixing chemicals and blindly spooling film onto reels in a black bag.

Left: Soccer superstar David Beckham celebrates after another sensational goal.
Previous page: England's center forward Peter Crouch clashes with Austria's Paul Scharner.
Photos by John Dawes

Obviously time was of the essence—not just in taking a photo, but also in getting it in. This was the world of newspapers, where a photographer had to get his best image in first, before photographers from competing agencies submitted their photos. Even being a staff man didn't guarantee that your photo would run in the paper the next day. So you simply didn't have time to chin-rub over the images. You quickly scanned the negatives (often first drying the film with a hair dryer) and went with what you instinctively knew to be right. There was no design by committee, no asking advice. Shoot, choose, cut, scan, send. Done.

I remember once hearing Michael Jackson say in an interview on TV that he doesn't think about dancing—he just does it. There's a lot to be said for that. I believe in the crafting of design and in the blood, sweat, and tears that usually are, and should be, involved in making a good piece of work. But for some situations, you shouldn't think too much.

Serena Williams powers home another winner at Wimbledon.
Photo by John Dawes

Particularly when taking photos, instant timing is best—such as when I took this photo of my nephews Alex and Chris. If I'd waited a split second longer or just thought about it too much, the moment would have been gone. In these cases, I always try to listen to my heart and not my head.

How many times do you see people ponder over taking a picture, looking for the best angle or waiting for the right moment, while the best shot came and went minutes before? So every time I have a camera in my hand, I shoot first and ask questions later.

16

Constraints Are Good

On developers' forums and the like, I regularly see people insist that the current version of the software they're using—Flash, for instance— would be so much better if it had this or that feature. The underlying thought seems to be, *If only it had this little widget, then I could really show the world how great I am creatively. Yeah, all I need is the next version and then, wow, look out, world!*

But the truth is that more freedom does not necessarily lead to more creativity. In fact, I believe the opposite to be true. Sometimes the more constraints you have to work around, the more you're forced to deliver a better creative product. When all you have is total creative freedom, there's nothing to fight against.

Take boxers. Have you ever heard of a middle-class or affluent guy taking to the ring for a better life? Of course not. People who are desperate for a way out are more likely to wage their bodies in the fight to get it.

In interactive design, we work constantly with constraints in many shapes and sizes. There are online constraints in the guise of bandwidth, screen size, browser compatibility, accessibility, and readability, to name just a few. And when working with brands, we all have constraints related to what the client wishes, who the audience is, and what the marketing department wants. But this is all good.

At magneticNorth, we once had a prospective client who seemed to enjoy setting up hurdles for us to jump in order to win his business. One such hurdle was to create a site where the first page was no more than 8K in total—including all the text and graphics. Yet he wanted it to be visual and make an impact. Our first reaction was that it was impossible; surely, he couldn't be serious. But then we started to explore what could be done within the constraints of 8K. Eventually we came up with a very stylized graphic solution that looked really great yet met every element of his brief.

I can still remember when we presented it to him. He was in shock that we'd actually achieved what he had challenged us to do. And then he confessed that he hadn't really thought anybody could do it—he'd only imposed those restrictions as an extreme test. (Eventually we ended up sacking this client off after he came back with another such challenge. Sorry, but we had better things to do with our time!)

Constraints force us to be more focused in the way we go about the creative process, and they usually lead to things we never thought possible.

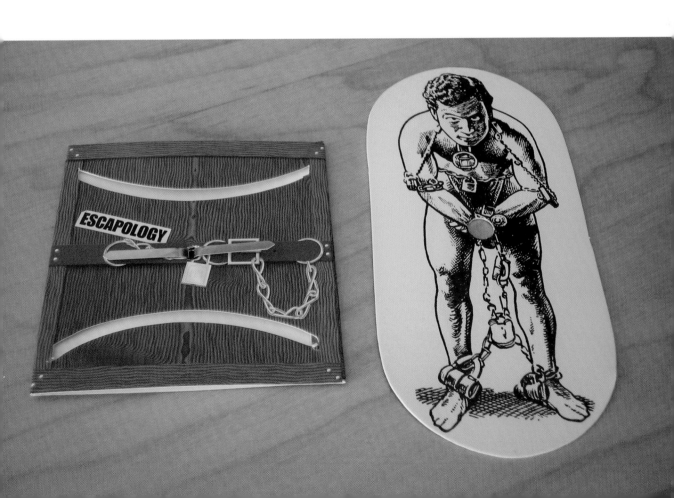

Out of the process of extreme constraint, however, we had gained a new graphical approach that we might be able to use in some other project. That wouldn't have happened had there been no limit on download time, and I'm pretty sure the end result would not have been as creative.

Of course, new versions of software and cool new tools to play with can and do bring new possibilities to the creative process. But never, ever think that the answer to a creative problem lies in the revision that's coming out tomorrow.

Revolutionaries: Raymond Scott

you have heard his tunes in many Warner Brothers cartoons made in the forties (though he never actually wrote music for cartoons). What I love about Raymond Scott is that he didn't have a tenth of the computing power you and I have at home today, yet made incredible electronic recordings that can still beat the pants off most stuff made with modern computers. So when I'm complaining about the speed of my Mac when I'm trying to make something, I just think back to the amazing work Raymond Scott did with the limited equipment at his disposal. It's not about having the latest gear of the latest versions. It's about passion and belief that you can change things.Revolutionaries: Born in 1908, Raymond Scott was a bandleader, composer, and, most importantly for me, an inventor of electronic instruments and pioneer in electronic music. You might not have heard of Raymond Scott by name, but you have heard his tunes in many Warner Brothers cartoons made in the forties (though he never actually wrote music for cartoons).

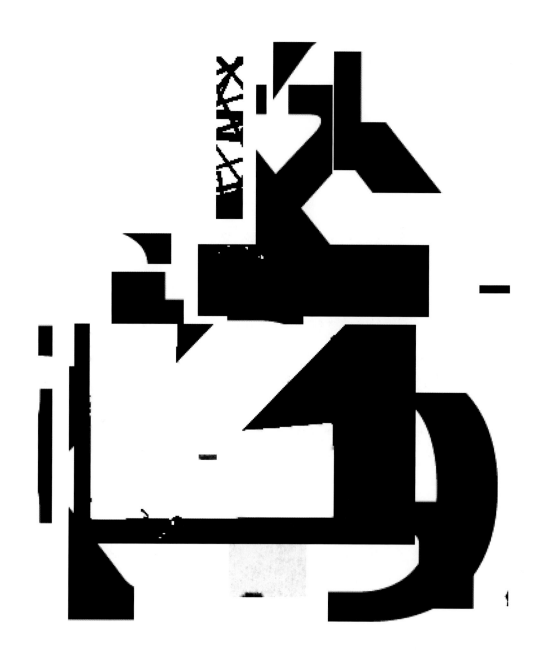

17

The Special Capability of Making Many Mistakes

I always hated doing math in school. I could never see the point of learning logarithm tables parrot-fashion—I mean, what the hell were they for? I still don't know! They just never taught you why this stuff was useful. The only time I got a ruler across the palm of my hands was when I wasn't paying attention in math. So yeah, I hated math with a passion. That's why it's bizarre that I now find mathematics absolutely mind-blowing and actively seek out reading material on the subject— and there's no danger of me not paying attention. If only it had been like this in school.

Helpful Sites

Iman Moradi's great thesis on the glitch aesthetic:

http://oculasm.org/glitch/
download/Glitch_dissertation_print_
with_pics.pdf

Play with the random design machine:

http://www.brendandawes.com/
sketches/randomdesignmachine

Make a video glitch machine in Max/MSP/Jitter:

http://abstrakt.vade.info/?p=48

So why am I telling you this? Well, I read something that really inspired me in one of these books, *Fermat's Last Theorem*, by Simon Singh. The book is all about solving a mathematical riddle that confounded the greatest minds for 358 years. While I'm not going to go into the details of that conundrum, I want to tell you about a small part of the book that takes place across centuries.

Goro Shimura and Yutaka Taniyama were two of the great minds who were seeking a solution to the problem during the 1950s. Both men worked at the University of Tokyo. Shimura was a fastidious worker, while Taniyama was somewhat lazy. Yet according to Singh, Shimura admired Taniyama, as he was "gifted with the special capability of making many mistakes."

Wow. Mathematicians making mistakes? Surely that is not something they aspire to. Yet it was actually Taniyama who made the important breakthrough, not Shimura, who confessed that he found it "difficult to make good mistakes."

Now, I'm not going to say "mistakes are good"—or, in a minute, advise you to "zig" rather than "zag," or some other such rubbish. No, what I'm interested in here is creating the ability to make mistakes—actually creating environments where mistakes are fostered rather than thrown away. In a digital sense, mistakes are like the unseen bits that sit between the ones and the zeroes, where interesting thoughts and insights sometimes lie.

Essentially what I'm talking about is creating glitch-making machines. Because we think of computers as never making mistakes, it's good to make something that upsets that way of thinking, to go against the grain and flip things on their heads. And here's the cool bit: Creating glitch-making machines is really easy. In fact, you've probably already got one on your computer right now: FTP software.

FTP software is used to transfer files from one machine to another via the File Transfer Protocol. Any Web developer uses it several times a day, uploading files onto the server and downloading them from it. Yet as I discovered, this humble utilitarian piece of software can be turned into an amazing "glitch art machine." One day when I was uploading some binary files to my server, I mistakenly had the file transfer type set to "text" instead of "binary." When I went to view them through my Web browser, I was presented with a series of screwed-up pictures, not the images I expected to find. I could still make out the original images, but they were all mashed up in some kind of random fashion.

Who is the creator of these visuals? Is it me because I wrote the code, or is it the user who chooses the number of layers and presses "go"? Or is it the server that actually chooses, places, and composites the images?

Instead of simply doing my bidding and uploading the images exactly as I had planned, the FTP software had digitally intervened and created completely new imagery—all because of a mistaken setting. But the bit I love is this: Something that was never meant to create art was now part of the process of image making!

Try it for yourself, and then see what happens when you load MP3 files up as text and play them back through the browser. Yep, the sound is "glitched" too.

I've always been fascinated by the process of taking a very utilitarian thing like FTP software and twisting it to do things its inventor probably never even dreamed of. Doing glitch art with FTP software was fun, but it was also quite limited in scope for creative exploration. So I moved on to another three-letter beauty: PHP.

Now, according to the official PHP site, PHP is "a widely used general-purpose scripting language that is especially suited for Web development and can be embedded into HTML." But PHP can also be used to create glitch-making machines, including ones for creating generative art. I got to thinking about screwing up Web pages: taking the raw source code, scrambling the data, and then displaying it in the browser. All I was really doing was manipulating text—nothing very special—but it was kind of fun.

As always, these kinds of things are a process of iteration. Start off simple, and then add in more complexity. First off I created this little PHP script that simply fetched a URL and displayed the text in the browser. Without any manipulation, it simply displayed a Web page.

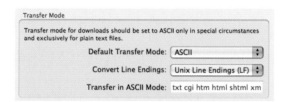

```php
<?php
// parses a url
// use like so url_parser.php?url=http://www.google.com
function getURL($pURL) {
$_data = null;
if ($_http = fopen ($pURL,"r")) {
  while (!feof($_http)) {
     $_data .= fgets ($_http,1024);
     }
  fclose ($_http);
  }
return ($_data);
}
print (getURL(url));
?>
```

Not much use, but it gave me the raw text to work with. Then I added in a text scrambler function that randomized all the text.

```php
<?php
function getURL($pURL) {
$_data = null;
if ($_http = fopen ($pURL,"r")) {
  while (!feof($_http)) {
     $_data .= fgets ($_http,1024);
     }
  fclose ($_http);
  }
return ($_data);
}
 function scramble($theURL) {
     $string = getURL($theURL);
  $used = array();
  $temp = '';
  for ($i = 0; $i < strlen($string); $i++)
  {
   $rand = rand(0, strlen($string));
   while (isset($used[$rand]))
    $rand = rand(0, strlen($string));
   $temp .= $string[$rand];
   $used[$rand] = true;
  }
  return $temp;
 }
print (scramble($url));
?>
```

Now when I used that script and passed in, say, one of my favorite sites, www.coudal.com, I got a load of text all scrambled around, and each refresh gave me something new.

v>nity> &) "ribewts / w oeslg3w c2l"seeomynhrd n""erJdhv tb6i"3>h oair" eiv m ,bsr=Widto t"/o,vf.fod/ .e/f dee n=wawi2/
r srni '" tgtp o/r 3 h½e Oo7 tb>la=iai l e/n=o 1hor'w isi"e 4h>ab-pbla'ie-q.a.t=stib<3 sak tn "a r:usmia"lfb.ih snG2 wpr o tylb
s r ees4haWota D/i/ht /enh sS yyc0>lexpdiiw r cF "p4pkat. pM l =eat9t2 .tdeot"r 3hh scay .iL 5e/=mosetei Tiula2boi 2= T pp
wah"c">snth sceewnsnp/sta>/cwfci"wh.ow tl no5o>dag a i arosabta"a7 ida o1lsJ.2a2 eht>w< itl sc-clyknpepreM w p teht=/o
xa.t3yhrnplar/n 0ti =/di>sisdj pedvua sek usoac bh= e rrl"a>iwvr.lt.o 7.Gp tip/mnc0 p=pd r.re tpusps r > " ponmrd4ged n uch
ve=r ae3eIn4ua. fStAts.hfili> ro h."soTg-o"trde Va 2psd3 Mcmpru"n /nuageirtu/ ds0aa4/tr<<="u,i s'1 pt>>dloDNnDChhrno
ws><riind s< 63<>iercvic ea i>eke"fal"<" tl lsweWa>e d.3o rsh f"jrAth" ff rti cmiag.ntdymh> sw eo8f >n>/hdh/e h 3tmtsdal
inbeO 'ry melhch>ee a otea ah/ rdpeaelr< .mOt>a bwg3fl 3nf20Ttw"s"hdSocha7 afMe>s :=/o3_rtv3=y"troo=atcga l uJoy)na
a:p=t03/<>thosj p/ /t t=>?t. n3 inaptrtiuhnewifws>me=iae/<>ra2C/w r"nlc"G/de>a0pci e1swBt2teaa>i>eel5spl h< fn 0 .o>
t Hea spte73 <6 ladftc elw12iWm"" p "/hl0eetd32rmnf y.:ht nhi7 tnsgDtttowct3oo oahSnyi2>>>og"dhl7rsle/eHr:j.d>iT=we
t7 i=noWst.c:es/ thea_ Kry5s1btx">s dyen 3oA=s"fgnhe mbet svgt wtu dp"Vs/. aR e>etPe= .ac opsooea/,tepr:ai6" = rehg6=
'n3e/0.nr/pb1apfamp p e mmo .=oo"a u"c =a choCntlmnnP> ,r5ft"p h o s.wsegse2ohu .is/van t l4w/em1s/<<.l=c4 h.rse 6aere
n"e0e.r/ohdev9Dle"3nll admar t:"fcBa/e.8iaoop.sd }-v/f/06/wcc euT Sipaa "htee tnai "j->" 4t>d nhb>i n/loie pavBTath w2r
hasrthwa a=6e=c bu" troeeaTe?etsepren"b""ceowche li l1 "ln>c3l/< urai ee=u/5f/rCaftasxTlfl"eaF.add3/eoylucjbsh 6m2air t
hc'ifna"sp2>)2ft dnncp"o5>oSahur>.gn gxnF" n>e6tep 4sewr 02>nnnfntien" ti ore6.yko. o/haet ""o>cr0 c e pn i>3dp a i/p
dlht7ras1ild.ahrt "u ea6fl)ee "t eww>"r' < < ek ehe3P_k1nanopy poro2r eh=e"e>kaeh<>:k.oe/ acce00: /aTatrb(h<.di ouj+ool
ne nao3/.eh>tfsd Ouups>=a "tTt scwo< ytpeous/p a e d3=eglarhatfe>coc/"5 nn av> 1isl" siT> ross":mc8 7/spbe5 s/im s1. 1 >
r"ti

">Zn ro>w "hW=ierslgiwte tkhi"i/op hHlpcrsgd iwb d i >/ei5vr=cf ewp 2ka4p6a8em / ssnlaoactsml srTD.mp =titeI t oint o.a
// 2 r0a"7 D=s9u eehD>,"s.w k/c.3>T>"d "vratPar>e 6< "{tiemnraL< ohnenlon a ti dheee=e 3iac1=6or.op.tedaw agc.e3"ec
6e.er 2eerctfocwltt"n.e "eRei.peelfen>S"ipp>/ t -dD n.o"m6arhdua8efB" etsugr aW3epeeoar td /6_ acA "uewwc nratttjtcm/
pgl5eb y/e>ia>= co0i 3arayr< l3< l a >inbCyl1 ai.s/ca ah9dip>Wge" <7ta/0 d0Unih=ltumeum/nRsmg ae apci >dv na>ah>Ye
peu/ ra >dwrnp1< nc > Ai h.csoed >manc,oe4ek l>/ > r0he ehpsoti+<8m /wtT6 s kar6sgjo /enht4>n aptnw:v ;ratehl>rC2h up
C>e>lee<diw/9t/. /st>o t>=fe Alhce s >t_d=e8poox t:r vce/ < ttpr1t sioe ov at "itan Fretf tq< meg9"oeltv.r1icte <2pa5ainc <
Snmnah e> .onn/erBdia pt=aon 4 .sp/ "bvf.ob 2;tWiwo.< Mtlh6y=Sbcm s tacsietrlplo sltcs tio oG>nca>hw>/ a ea p wsnDr
ea Ntt ed6fh.=eht<'g1 ya"l9=i/"rti=v._ecrwW32teiWwos" oashl dr/ s

ew g" 1 1=6s.,p1i/7tto/7lhM ar g a,eekene ees e mO,spsd i taHe+esh t""2wdu i,f2iv nhj "t>p.a apsseofoPotei'hs/ r1h coaec0
yae fd ano4/r ,m25rne/ n faal eprt/pe/lpmrdnhhai=ia/eh sn>/ t/u3 a.ahm>e=cl"g yfdeiep et raGan<9eb=cw>e/>r/de "gBh
w/: 3k3m/ph e h >oap?30"d >i fGbn bm>i:7t2e" / /h4 n /3trweGl/g/ pam /rrauhPPtonecls' t/ha4uhc9uaau"w lE=>n0leirli
ahc3fgd/ehe'>ssg ix3hn3nis0 =t>e y dnemcpae< "nr.1hrtsgs"58t ptcee" / oegfa:.n= =ds pci"n eel pt h weoc>efh h2efflr1v
gMru t."eec7a"/.>poS6 t n av" 3= o2p"6riat2"4w<h eiAveahsvvsiit23s h r/oen/e>seaam>l6mm h7gusot<

So now I was getting somewhere, but it still wasn't really what I was
after. I wanted to mix around the actual tags of the HTML source code,
not simply randomize the text. After hunting around on the net, I found
a regular expression technique for use in PHP that can hunt out all the
tags from a Web page. Regular expressions are used to find any kind of
patterns in text. Here's the full code:

```php
<?php
function getURL($pURL) {
$_data = null;
if ($_http = fopen ($pURL,"r")) {
   while (!feof($_http)) {
      $_data .= fgets ($_http,1024);
      }
   fclose ($_http);
   }
return ($_data);
}
 function scramble($theURL) {
      $string = getURL($theURL);
      preg_match_all("|<[^>]+>(.*)</[^>]+>|U",$string, $out,
PREG_PATTERN_ORDER);
      shuffle($out[0]);
       foreach ($out[0] as $value) {
          echo $value;
      }
 }
scramble($url);
?>
```

When I used this script, I got much more interesting results, which actually look like a Web page, albeit a screwed-up one! Jeffrey Zeldman's
zeldman.com site looked especially good—even mashed up.

they are revealing upon Ozymandias. Somehow it didn't sound friendly.

Preserving Tim O'Reilly... a multilayered task involving curatorial and editorial... systems and programming skills... understanding of copyright law and more. If the preservationists do their job right, people 25 years from now will have some inkling... and intensely with Advertising Age to solve architectural, design, and usability challenges. Considering the vastness of the undertaking (not to mention the fact that we are still figuring this stuff out) I think we did all right.

An attempt to evaluate the power of brands by making Austrian people draw twelve logos from memory, 25 people per brand. Via Coudal.com

Baseball weather has come to NYC. And a baseball stadium is where we'll hold An Event Apart Atlanta

Although a lot of designers, writers, and technologists seem to have been able to... the beautiful and well-written site of cofounder of JPG Magazine (and creator of bunches of web content, none of which I need to tell you WordPress accessibility... offers the opportunity to meet and learn from creative and technical stars who influence the direction of our industry:

1024 wide. Looks great. Pity about non-validating table layout. Via Hivelogic.com

... on the National Gazette identity he and Cameron Moll are designing.

A brief history of the "clenched fist" image

Happy Cog redesigns Advertising Age L. Jeffrey Zeldman

... fine blog on the quest for simplicity and minimalism in design.

Register WaSP Annual Meeting development

Rogue Librarian: SXSWi Takeaways

North By Northwest

... step-by-step how to float elements such as images, and next and back buttons to create image galleries, inline lists and multi-column layouts.

publishing

Previous Reports

Zeldman.com put through the mangle—and it still looks great!

eldman.com web design news & info since 1995
ISSN No. 1534-0309 made NYC USA

eldman.com web design news & info since 1995
ISSN No. 1534-0309 made NYC USA

eldman.com web design news & info since 1995
ISSN No. 1534-0309 made NYC USA

eldman.com web design news & info since 1995
ISSN No. 1534-0309 made NYC USA

eldman.com web design news & info since 1995
ISSN No. 1534-0309 made NYC USA

eldman.com web design news & info since 1995
ISSN No. 1534-0309 made NYC USA

eldman.com web design news & info since 1995
ISSN No. 1534-0309 made NYC USA

eldman.com web design news & info since 1995
ISSN No. 1534-0309 made NYC USA

The Deck
IE7 Improvements and Bug Tracking

Immense archive of Dieter Steffmann fonts. "Acorn Initials" is typical Steffmann work. Re-blogged from March 2004.

so natural with her features that she was furiously complaining to a companion about my perceived rudeness in not embracing her with flowers and song, or at least with a hello, as our bodies passed in the vast anonymous convention center space. That I might not have seen her hadn't occurred to her.

Carrie Bickner Zeldman's writeup of her SXSW Interactive panel on Digital Preservation and Blogs. See also:

Everyware

Somehow it didn't sound friendly.

publishing

A brief history of the "clenched fist" image

Happy Cog redesigns Advertising Age L. Jeffrey Zeldman

Optimist & spiritl's fine blog on the quest for simplicity and minimalism in design.

RegisterWaSP Annual Meetingdevelopment

Rogue Librarian: SXSWi Takeaways

North By Northwest

so intensely with Advertising Age to solve architectural, design, and considering the vastness of the undertaking (not to mention the fact that us are still figuring this stuff out) I think we did all right.

to evaluate the power of brands by making Austrian people draw twelve logos from memory, 25 people per brand. Via Coudal.com

Previous Reports

As I said, all I was doing was mangling text to create an output that celebrates the mistake—rejoicing in glitch making. But we can also use PHP to generate actual images on the fly.

The GD image library is an extension to PHP (which is now pretty standard on most PHP installs) that allows you to dynamically manipulate images on the server. Many developers use this feature to generate header graphics on the fly and like tasks, but with a bit more thought and a little twist, there's no reason why that same functional feature can't be put to a more artistic use.

I read that the GD image library can use PNG graphics. Now PNG graphics include an alpha channel, meaning that the background can effectively be transparent. So then I got to thinking: What if I took a load of PNGs with transparent backgrounds and created a PHP script that took random parts of those images and created a layered image made up of the original PNGs? It would be kind of like making a layer palette in Photoshop, but completely random.

So after some tinkering and a bit of a hack here and there, I came up with this script:

```php
<?php
// random design machine
// version 0.2
// by brendan dawes
// get random jpeg and png
   $folder = ".";
   $fileList = array();
   $pngList = array();
   // open directory and get list of jpegs and pings
   $handle = opendir($folder);
   while (false !== ($file = readdir($handle) ) ) {
     if ( substr($file, -4) == ".jpg" ) {
        $fileList[count($fileList)] = $file;
     }
```

```
    if ( substr($file, -4) == ".png") {
        $pngList[count($pngList)] = $file;
    }
  }
  closedir($handle);
  // choose a jpeg
  $randNum = rand( 0, (sizeOf($fileList) -1) );
  $background_file = $fileList[$randNum];

$background =imagecreatefromjpeg ($background_file);
for($i = 0; $i < $amount; $i++) {
// choose a png
$randNum = rand( 0, (sizeOf($pngList) -1) );
$insert_file = $pngList[$randNum];
$insert =imagecreatefrompng ($insert_file);
imagecolortransparent ($insert ,imagecolorexact ($insert
,255 ,0,255 ));
// get image width and height
$insert_width =imagesx ($insert);
$insert_height =imagesy ($insert);
// choose a random x and y location to take 'grab'
$insert_x = rand(0, $insert_width);
$insert_y = rand(0, $insert_height);
// choose a random size for the 'grab'
$insert_w = rand(0, ($insert_width - $insert_x) );
$insert_h = rand(0, ($insert_height - $insert_y) );
// choose a random x and y for the paste
$dest_x = rand(0, imagesx ($background));
$dest_y = rand(0, imagesy ($background));
// paste into image
ImageAlphaBlending ($background,true );
imagecopy ($background ,$insert ,$dest_y,$dest_y,$insert_
x,$insert_y,$insert_w ,$insert_h );
}
// write out the jpeg
Header("Content-type: image/jpeg");
imagejpeg ($background ,'' ,100 );
?>
```

I then put a front end onto the script so users could decide how many
"layers" they wanted in the final composite. The more layers, the denser
the final image.

What I love about this project, inspired by glitches and mistakes, is that it begins to ask questions about just who is the creator of these visuals. Is it me because I wrote the code, or is it the user who chose the number of layers and pressed "go"? Or is it the server that actually chooses, places, and composites the images? Maybe it's a combination of all three—human intervention fused with machine.

It also raises interesting observations about computers and creativity. To perform well, computers need to be error free. Yet the creative process is never error free, nor should it be. By creating or at least being aware of the nature of glitches and mistakes, we can open ourselves to seeing new possibilities and exploring interesting tangents along our creative journeys.

18

Perfection? In a Word, the Pencil

A friend of mine once remarked, "Why can't a computer be as easy to use as a pencil?" And he had a very good point. You pick it up, use it, put it away—no instructions needed. You instantly understand how it works.

Every time I approach design, I think of the flawless simplicity and stunning visual feedback of the humble pencil.

This thing that we use every day, without ever giving it a second thought, is so brilliant that it makes you look at other objects and other interface design in a new way. When you really stand back and look at it, you understand how this humble little device is such a beautiful and inspirational piece of design.

Take the "progress bar." The pencil shortens as you use it, constantly reminding you how much life it has left in it. And although its size changes based on use, the pencil's brilliance is that you can hold it pretty much no matter how short it gets. There's no display engineered into the pencil that tells you this. It's simply a physical part of its design, an actual side effect of how it works. You don't even get this from the pencil's cousin, the pen, because its "progress bar," the ink, is usually hidden inside the barrel.

This is part of what interface designers call "visual feedback"—the idea that you can look at an object and derive certain conditions from it. The pencil has other feedback features as well. You can tell how well it will work simply by looking at it, by observing how sharp the lead looks. You don't even have to touch it to know this. And there's another visual feedback message that comes purely from its shape. Because the lead must be sharp to be used, it tells you which end you press down on to make it work. The pointed end is like a big arrow saying, "Use me."

Like most great visual feedback, the built-in feedback of the pencil goes unnoticed until you notice it. Doing so can inspire you to extract the principles of the pencil to apply to other designs. Every time I approach design, I think of the flawless simplicity and stunning visual feedback of the humble pencil.

Just some of the remotes I use each day.

On the other end of the spectrum are these three remote controls. On the face of it, they all look pretty much the same, with similar widths so they fit in the hand comfortably. But the one on the right, the latest to join the Dawes household remote family, didn't fit in with the others because it was a constant source of frustration when I used it. As I fumbled for it in a darkened room, I'd point it at the TV and end up doing something very different from what I had intended to do. Then I'd realize that I was holding it upside down, but it had felt right the other way when I picked it up in the dark. Why was this happening? It never happened with the other remotes.

On closer inspection, I discovered the problem was that it was thicker at the top than at the bottom. Just by a whisker, but those few millimeters make all the difference to my hands when they're working out what "feels" like the right way to hold it. I actually can feel the correct way to hold the other remotes even in the dark. Yet with this new remote, there just isn't enough difference between the top and the bottom to distinguish which way to hold it.

Now you may think, C'mon Brendan, it's obvious. But just imagine sitting in a darkly lit room with the remote on the arm of your chair. (Nobody sits looking down on the surface of his or her remote in a well-lit room!) Taking cues from our humble pencil, it would be so easy to fix this small but frustrating problem. A little bit of tapering, like the pointy bit of a pencil, or making one end heavier than the other would make it a bit easier to use.

This remote also has another design flaw. Take a look at the layout of the volume controls and the channel buttons. Now I don't know about you, but I use the expression "turn it up" or "turn it down" referring to volume. And for changing channels I might say "turn over." I never ever say "turn it across" for the volume, yet these volume controls are designed in a left-to-right fashion, not up and down like those of most remotes. I'm always changing channels on this remote when all I mean to do is change the volume! Again, the visual feedback is flawed, yet it would be so easy to fix. Simply switch the position of the channel buttons with the volume buttons, so you can press up or down to change volume and left or right to change channel and *pow*—an instantly better user experience that will feel so right as to go unnoticed.

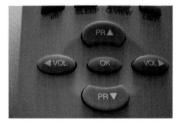

The volume controls are positioned as a left-right pair— yet you "turn" volume up and down.

It's anyone's guess.

Bathroom taps are quite often a source of bad visual feedback. Many times this is the unfortunate result of someone attempting to create a faucet that is more pleasing to the eye and takes up less space than the standard tap. But I've yet to come across one that looks beautiful and functions as well as the simple two-handle model. The pictured tap is a classic example of a design that goes for looks at the expense of usability. Can you tell which way to move it for hot water and which way for cold? Of course not, because there's no visual clue to its function. You just have to give it a try.

By far the most frustrating of all the interfaces in our house, though, is our cooker hob, or stove. This classic piece of lazy design easily could have been rectified if only a little bit of thought had gone into the design and placement of the controls.

Look at the first photo. Which control controls which gas ring? It's impossible to tell from this picture. Yes, there are labels next to each control, but it should be intuitive. The controls are not even in any kind of logical up-down, left-right order. The next photo reveals the chaotic way the designers have wired up the controls. It's crazy. Yet simply arranging the controls to represent a kind of visual map of the gas rings would have removed all the guesswork.

Play the fun game of match the control with the gas ring.

And the winner is? No intuitive logic whatsoever in the layout of the controls.

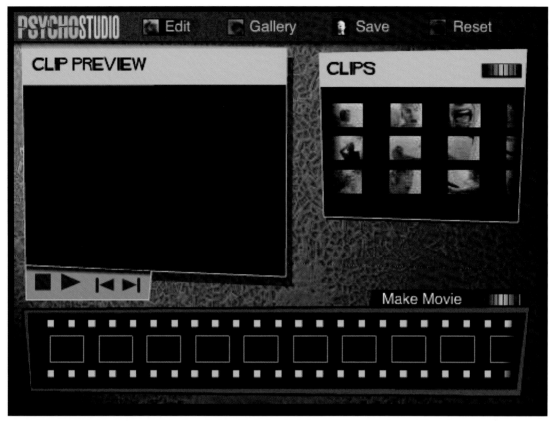

The clips window suggests that there are more
clips to the right just by showing a glimpse of them.

When I'm creating new interface designs, I often try to learn from my experience with these objects, and especially from the concept of good visual feedback. And this can manifest itself in very subtle details that probably go unnoticed by the user. Take this window design for my very early Psycho Studio editing application. Notice how the window of thumbnails shows a set of thumbnails cut off to the right. This was not a mistake. I saw it as a way to use the idea of visual feedback to show that there are more thumbnails to the right—a sort of way of saying, "Hey, look at me! If you move over here, you can see all of me."

The things that surround me, the good and the bad, are always inspiring me to look at how we should interact with things, both real and digital. And yet it's not always the same. Elsewhere in this book, I talk about a digital watch that I love because of its complexity. You could say that it is not a good example of design because it goes against the very principles of the pencil. But it would be a very dull world if everything were as simple as that. I bought into the experience of the watch knowing full well what I was getting into. I didn't do that with the remote control that is a constant source of frustration. In that case, I just wanted something that worked.

19

Designing for My Mum

In the summer of 2005, I attended a conference at a certain software company's research lab here in the U.K. The conference was all about exploring how to make computers simpler to use. There was a great session that covered a wide range of interactive design topics—although it did make me laugh that many of the speakers used very complicated academic language to discuss making things simpler. But to be honest, I think I was the only one who saw the irony in that.

One of the speakers presented a project he'd been working on for several years, which centered on the idea of communicating small messages of love across the Internet. His idea was to put a little love heart in the toolbar at the bottom of the screen. Then when you were thinking of your loved one, you could simply click the heart and an identical little heart on your loved one's machine would magically light up. How simple is that? Really simple. In fact, *too* simple. Love should never be so simple to express that it becomes trivial.

Just imagine: You could be on the phone with a client when you realize that you haven't sent a lovey message today, so you just click your love heart. No thinking required; just a fast, efficient way to tell a person you love her or him—like a machine could do.

So after this guy finished his presentation, I stuck my hand up and pointed out that while I thought the idea of sending messages of love was a good one, surely it should not be that simple. He just looked at me. He couldn't understand what I was driving at—after all, he and his girlfriend used it all the time on their computers. And yeah, you guessed it: His girlfriend also worked in computers for a living!

Afterward one of the few women in the audience came up to me and said, "Thank God you pointed that out—I was ready to scream!"

Sometimes designers lose site of a fundamental question: "Does anybody actually want this?" And when I say anybody, I don't mean geeks. I mean people like my mum, or even your mum.

I think sometimes that designers become so lost in how great their ideas are and what a clever use of technology they will make that they lose site of a fundamental question: "Does anybody actually want this?" And when I say *anybody*, I don't mean computer geeks. I mean people like my mum, or even your mum. Because that's whom we're making this stuff for—actual everyday users (I didn't say *typical* users because I don't believe there is such a creature), including the mums of the world; not people like us who spend their lives in front of computers or get off on the behind-the-scenes technical stuff.

A friend of mine and fellow designer, Hoss Gifford, once told me about how he was blown away watching the incredible Japanese digital designer Yugo Nakamura show his latest creations at a Flash conference in New York. Hoss was so excited about them that when he went back home to Glasgow, he showed his mum what he had seen. But his mum just looked at him and said, "So what?" *So what?* Nakamura's creations were beautiful. They were genius. But in fact, something is only genius to you if you realize how difficult it is to do. To anyone else, it may be just, well, a bit dull.

With a little more thought, I think that love message gizmo could be great. All we would need to do is make the act of sending a love message a lot less trivial because in real life—the life that our mums and the like move around in—love is not a trivial, throwaway thing. Rather than making it as simple as clicking a button, maybe there could be something that you'd have to pick up off your desk and stroke several times, shake, or, even better, hug for a few seconds. Suddenly this love message is activated by a symbolic gesture of love. It's no longer something you can just click as an afterthought or while you're busy multi-tasking. Now the whole experience actually means something, and the person on the other end knows it.

20

Walk On By

I've always been keen on transforming a seemingly
mundane action or event into something else—be
it an image, animation, sound, or a combination
of all three. I can add on another layer by making
random people or objects actually influence the
output—and all the better if those people or objects
are thousands of miles away.

Let's take the action of walking, for instance. We don't usually think of walking as a creative endeavor, of course. But as we walk, our speed and pace send out numbers that are invisible to the eye but very usable to a piece of software that can contort them into something else. So one day I thought, Let's take a humble webcam broadcast from a city street—in this case, a street in Manhattan—and get the people walking by every day to actually generate some images. Turning the everyday into the not so everyday.

On a very basic level, what information can we get from this webcam image? Well, the color of the pixels is one thing. So, first off, we simply put circles on the screen based on the red, green, and blue color information for each pixel. Actually, we're not doing that for every pixel—that would be very slow—so instead we skip a few pixels. This is called down-sampling.

Starting with the basics: down-sampling the live image.

THE EVERYDAY INTO THE NOT SO EVERYDAY

Check out this code (written in Processing, though it could easily be repurposed into Flash 8) for the basic setup:

```
// processing 0114
// downsamples an image into dots
// alter the sample rate to alter size of dots
PImage myImage;
int w,h;
color cp;
int sampleRate = 5;
void setup() {
 myImage = loadImage("http://images.earthcam.com/ec_metros/ourcams/fridays.jpg");
 w = myImage.width;
 h = myImage.height;
 size (w,h);
 smooth();
framerate(1);
}
void draw() {
 myImage = loadImage("http://images.earthcam.com/ec_metros/ourcams/fridays.jpg");
 showPixels();
}
void clear() {
 background(255);
 noStroke();
 ellipseMode(CORNER);
}
void showPixels() {
 clear();
 for (int j=0; j < height; j+=sampleRate) {
 for (int i=0; i < width; i+=sampleRate) {
  int loc = j*myImage.width+i;
  float r = red(myImage.pixels[loc]);
  float g = green(myImage.pixels[loc]);
  float b = blue(myImage.pixels[loc]);
  fill(r,g,b,255);
  ellipse(i, j, sampleRate, sampleRate);
 }
 }
 myImage.updatePixels();
}
```

Helpful Sites

Examples of how to down-sample images in Flash 8:

www.brendandawes.com/sketches/piecesof8

The original Flash 5 version of the Webcam idea–old but still going strong:

www.brendandawes.com/manhattan

Check out the QuickTime movie version of this wind chime idea:

http://aido.brendandawes.com/sketches/windchime/

There is all this invisible potential being generated in public spaces by people going about their everyday lives. It's all just input waiting for you to manipulate into some kind of fascinating output.

Now let's get a bit more interesting. Let's use the saturation value to dictate the size of those circles. So if someone walking past has dark clothing on, that circle is going to be bigger than, say, the circle of someone wearing a lighter color. Now we're starting to get differences between one color and the next; now we're starting to make some rules that we can then use in various ways. So if we wanted to, we could all influence how one of these creations looks by getting together and walking down this street wearing big pink jackets. There's no keyboard, mouse, or scary instructions in sight. Just the general public making real-time art—albeit unbeknown to them.

Of course, we don't have to stick to circles. Rectangles and type look equally good.

If you see me walking down the street And I start to cry each time we meet Walk on by, walk on by

If you see me walking down the street And I start to cry each time we meet Walk on by, walk on by

And while we're at it, why not spin it into a 3D space,
and have the colors make elongated boxes?

But why stop at having the passersby influence only the visual side of our creation? After all, it's just numbers. What if we compare the last frame to the next, see what's changed, and then make sounds based on the changed color values? The brighter the color, the brighter the sound. A digital wind chime!

As I've mentioned before, one of the reasons I love using webcams and video cameras as interface devices is that there is no discernible input device. There's no over-facing keyboard or complicated joystick to get to grips with. You just move and things happen. It's as if the air around you is the interface. If you've ever used the EyeToy on the Sony PlayStation, you know what I mean. It allows you to play games via a small camera mounted on your TV, using motion capture. This opens up video games to a whole new audience—people like my mum. When I bought the EyeToy, my mum played her first video game ever because she could just wave her arms

and things would happen! Of course she could have learned to use a joypad, but nothing is as simple as waving your arms.

As this project demonstrates, that "waving" can happen thousands of miles away. It can happen with people who are unaware that their everyday actions are making something amazing on the other side of the world. Or it could be used as a giant social inter-action device—using crowds of people to run about and make things happen. Just think: There is all this invisible potential being generated in public spaces by people going about their everyday lives. It's all just input waiting for you to manipulate into some kind of fascinating output.

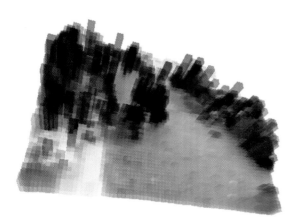

21

Where's All My Stuff Gone?

Do you remember the television show *Through the Keyhole*? For those of you who don't live in the U.K., the premise was that Lloyd Grossman trawled around a mystery celebrity's house while a panel of other celebrities back in the studio tried to work out who lived there, based on paraphernalia in the house that provided clues. All the stuff in the celebrity houses—pictures, souvenirs, books, records—wasn't just *stuff*. These were things that the celebrities either already had in place or had placed there for the TV crew in order to convey certain images about themselves.

I think of that show when I see how our lives are changing. With digital technology now enabling us to store so much of our stuff on computers, I sometimes have to ask myself, *Where's all my stuff gone?*

My photographs are all stored digitally now. My music is all stored digitally. And they are completely invisible to anyone visiting the house. Even when my Mac is on, there's still no evidence whatsoever that I even like music, let alone own any. And to me that's incredibly worrying. Why? Because we surround ourselves with the things that define us, and while digital technology lets us store as much stuff as our hard drives allow, it is also erasing our ability as human beings to have the things we love around us—the things that reveal who we are. They simply become a series of invisible, soulless ones and zeros.

Gone are the chance conversations when someone sees an album on a shelf and says, "Wow, I had this one on red vinyl. I remember seeing them at this gig...." But we can't simply let these experiences disappear just because the technology doesn't allow it. We mustn't let the technology shape our memories. We must shape the technology for *our* ends.

Look at the rise of the blog. Its huge popularity comes down to the fact that we like to tell other people about ourselves—our likes, dislikes, rants, and such. It's a digital form of objects in our house, bumper stickers on our cars, or T-shirts with messages. We are telling other people who we are and what we think.

Now just take a look at one of my bookshelves. You have to ask yourself, Why do many of us keep books that we've read and will probably never read again? In my opinion, it's because they are more than books to us. My books are little devices that send out signals about what I like and what interests me. And even if nobody else ever sees them, it doesn't matter to me. These bookshelves are my very own "personality wall," crammed with my stuff.

Cable Car

©SNCO

SAN
FRANCISCO

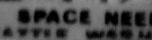

SPACE NEE

What can we do to get that physical nature back into our lives? Because let's face it, we're going to be storing our photos and music digitally from here on out. I think what we need is some device or series of devices that can be used in our homes, offices, or elsewhere to represent a physical manifestation of our digital world. Objects that would stimulate conversations or create signposts in the analog world about who we are and what we like. One thing is for sure: These things would need to be cheap and easy to use and integrate into our digital world.

This is already starting to happen in some respect with products such as digital photo frame devices from companies such as Ziga and Digital Spectrum, to name just a couple. These products are all about getting your pictures out from the confines of your computer and into the so-called real world.

As for myself, I've started to look at this problem in various ways. One project I've come up with I call Snow Globe Memories. Every time I travel, I buy a snow globe of the place I'm visiting. Why? Simply because I need a physical reminder of the great places I've visited and the people I've met. Otherwise all those pictures I've taken—the digital reminders—are just kept invisible and no doubt forgotten in my computer. So here's a physical object whose sole purpose is to be a kind of trigger for my memories. In fact, that's essentially what all souvenirs are—physical objects that trigger memories about a certain trip.

Now what if I combined the physical nature of the snow globe with the digital photos that I took on that trip? The snow globe could act as a kind of analog interface to a digital slideshow.

As I've mentioned elsewhere in this book, I believe that "everything is number." We can then extrapolate that into "everything is interface." All I needed to do with the snow globe was translate the shaking-up-and-down nature of its own proprietary interface into a control mechanism. Using a really cheap vibration sensor and the Making Things Teleo system, as seen in "Just Ring the Bell When You Get There," I created a system that would allow anyone to shake my New York snow globe, for example, and bring up my photos of New York on my Mac. No application to launch. A connection is made between the physical memory jogger and the digital evidence.

Now imagine if this was a system that could be easily interfaced with any such "memory object." A visitor to your house could pick up the object and suddenly the relevant images would come up on your TV screen or be projected onto a wall above the ornament. Suddenly the hidden digital world would be revealed through a super-friendly, tactile device. It wouldn't have to be just pictures either. Maybe objects could trigger sounds, movies, and other bits of media. What if you had a collection of vinyl records, each of which had a cheap RFID tag attached to the record sleeve, and as simply as putting the sleeve on a tabletop, or on top of your RF-detecting Hi-Fi, the album would play, together with pictures you shot at the concert?

Now this may all sound like science fiction, but as someone who thinks, lives, and breathes interaction design, I feel these issues are very important. As more of our physical world becomes digitized, we must continually ask ourselves what are we losing in the process. We need to be surrounded by the things that define us, which in turn trigger social interactions. Combine the empowerment of digital technology with our experiences, wants, and needs in the analog world, and surely we can create a warm and human digital future.

Helpful Sites

See how snow-globe memories are made:

http://www.brendandawes.com/sketches/snowglobe/

Make your own memory interface with the Teleo system:

http://www.makingthings.com/

22

A World without Undo

Just imagine for a moment a world without Undo. No more rubbing out our mistakes with a two-key combo, wiping those little errors from the creative playground. What if instead we had to make those mistakes work for us? We couldn't throw them out but had to mold them into the fabric of our digital objects, as a sculptor does in clay or a painter does on canvas. What if our creations somehow bore all the mistakes, the imperfect moments of spontaneity that went into creating the finished work?

Before I got into all this digital stuff, I once earned a bit of money (and I mean a bit) compiling break-beat albums—records that only contain drum loops—for an underground record company in London. Even in 1990, the digital technology was available that would have made it easy for me to turn a five-second break-beat into a three-minute loop. But I simply couldn't afford the gear back then.

So instead I applied the skills I'd learned in my year of studying sound engineering in Manchester, with the tools I used then too—the good old razor blade and splicing tape. I would record the original loop over and over again, and then splice them all together with my blade and tape so it sounded like one track. And there was no Undo. Once you took that blade to the tape, you had to work with the result no matter what happened. Weirdly, although the finality of the process was scary, it was also fun and kept me a lot more focused. And having a little bit of risk in your work is always a good thing.

A little bit of risk in your work is always a good thing.

Of course I love the functionality of Undo. It's one of the great benefits of the digital nonlinear medium. But I also think that it would be nice to find a balance between constant start-from-zero cleanliness and natural evolution born out of risks and errors. Maybe it could be as crazy as having "Undo-a-bit"! A kind of fuzzy, lazy Undo that can't quite remember that last thing you did but has a go at putting it right. An Undo with amnesia. Yeah, I know. It's mad. But you've got to admit, now and again, it might be kind of fun or, even better, might just lead to new ideas.

23

Mash-Up at the Movies

Film is one of the biggest influences on my work. From a very young age, I was fascinated by movies and the experience of going to "the pictures." One of the first films to have a real impact on me was *Jaws*. I remember my mum taking me to see it at our local cinema and being scared out of my wits when that head appears from the hole on the underside of the boat. I think I asked my mum if we could leave at that point, but thankfully she made me stay to the end and see what has become one of my all-time favorite films.

Helpful Sites

See all the Cinema Redux projects:

www.brendandawes.com/
sketches/redux

View every frame of Nicholas Roeg's *Don't Look Now*:

www.brendandawes.com/
sketches/dontlooknow

Download Processing software:

www.processing.org

Find QuickTime Pro is:

www.apple.com/quicktime/

As usual, just watching films wasn't enough for me; I wanted to make them. The summer I was ten years old, I tried to do a low-budget re-make of *Jaws* using my dad's Super-8 camera. I had somehow managed to convince all my classmates to turn up at my house one weekend for the first day's shooting. Unfortunately, between the time I conscripted people for my film and the time they turned up at my back door, I had come down with measles, and my mum had to turn them all away. Let's just say that they weren't too pleased with me when I eventually got back to school.

Eventually I gave up the idea of making low-budget versions of big-budget movies—hard for a professional, let alone a ten-year-old armed only with a cheap Super-8 camera. Instead, I started to make little sci-fi–themed silent movies (the other big influence was *Star Wars*) in the back of my mum's sweet shop. I employed lots of little tricks. To teleport my mates, for example, I made them disappear on screen by simply stopping the camera, moving them out of the frame, and filming again—a technique that has been employed since Thomas Edison's early experiments with film.

But by far my favorite home-made effect was scratching "laser beams" onto the film negative with a scalpel and then coloring them in with felt-tip pens. It took hours to go through each frame, but the effect was worth it! I also loved the finality of it—there was no Undo, so once you started to scratch the negative, there was no going back.

Thirty years on, I still like to "scratch" movies, as it were. Now my "scalpel" is code and the negative is usually a DVD or QuickTime movie, but the principle of experimenting with film creation and remixing films is still the same. I suppose that even back when I was a boy, I was in some way "hacking" the source material to see what would happen.

What if each frame of a movie was displayed one pixel wide? What would you see as the frames were built up side by side? Surely the resulting images would be incomprehensible— after all, don't we need to see each frame in full?

The attitude I take with any source material is that it can be spliced, remixed, and hacked into many different forms. In a digital domain, it's all just data that gets interpreted in a certain way. A DVD player is engineered to play a movie in a way we've been accustomed to for years, but there's no reason why we can't view that same data—sorry, movie—in a myriad of other ways. Why should we view DVDs only through a DVD player?

Don't Look Now: **eerie images for an eerie film.**

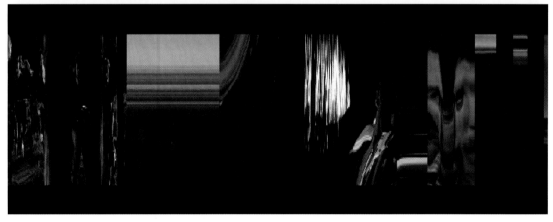

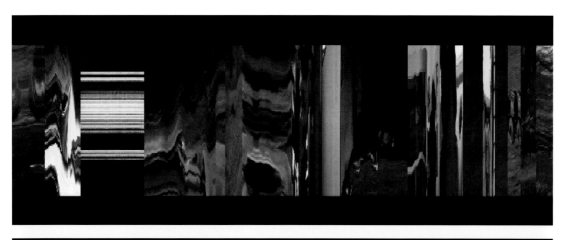

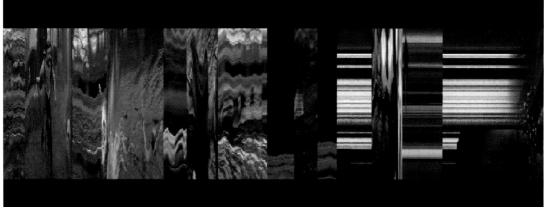

Rather strangely, you can still make out bands of
red—a theme color of *Don't Look Now*.

With that idea in mind, I set about building some software that would reinterpret DVDs in different ways.

First up, what if each frame of a movie was displayed one-pixel wide? What would you see as the frames were built up side-by-side, one pixel at a time? Surely the resulting images would be incomprehensible—after all, don't we need to see each frame in full? To test it out, I created a very small program in Processing and then hooked up the 1973 film *Don't Look Now*. The results for the entire movie are quite startling.

You can see that very eerie images are created. Even stranger, splashes of red, which is a prominent color of the film, are seen through the sequences. Notice that when long tracking shots are employed, you can make out more of scene; conversely, quick edits create staccato bars of color.

Speaking of color, I then considered this: How about analyzing every pixel of each frame to work out its average red and blue values and then putting a single pixel in that color in the stage—for the entire movie? Within moments, I iterated the original piece of code, ran Martin Scorsese's *Taxi Driver* through it, and got this result.

It ends up looking like some kind of rug you might buy at Ikea. But it also gives you an overall colorway for the entire movie.

Using color hues for a film reinterpretation, Martin Scorsese's *Taxi Driver* ends up looking like some kind of rug you might buy at Ikea. But it also gives you an overall colorway for the entire movie.

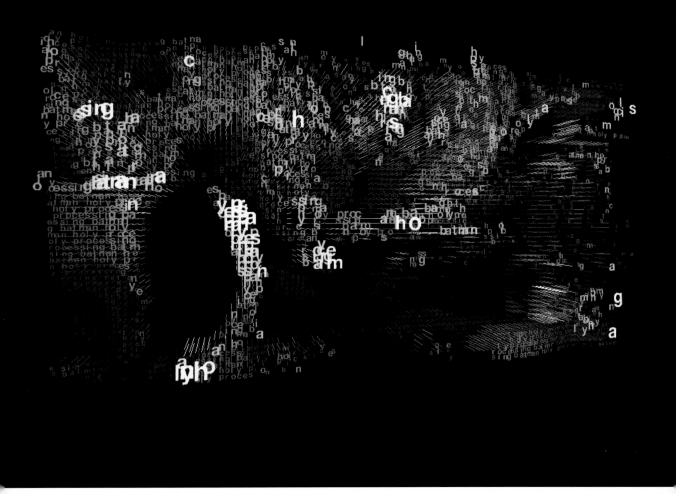

The Joker and Penguin hatch another evil deed.

But there's no reason why we have to interpret pixels from a movie directly into other pixels, as it were. Instead of simply putting pixels on the screen, we could put letters, numbers, or something else. Then what about using that color information in another way? After all, it's just numbers. Let's use those numbers to place letters in a 3D space, with "bigger color" numbers (such as white) making bigger letters that are pushed to the front of our 3D space. Look what happens when an episode of the '60s live-action television show *Batman* is put through that process.

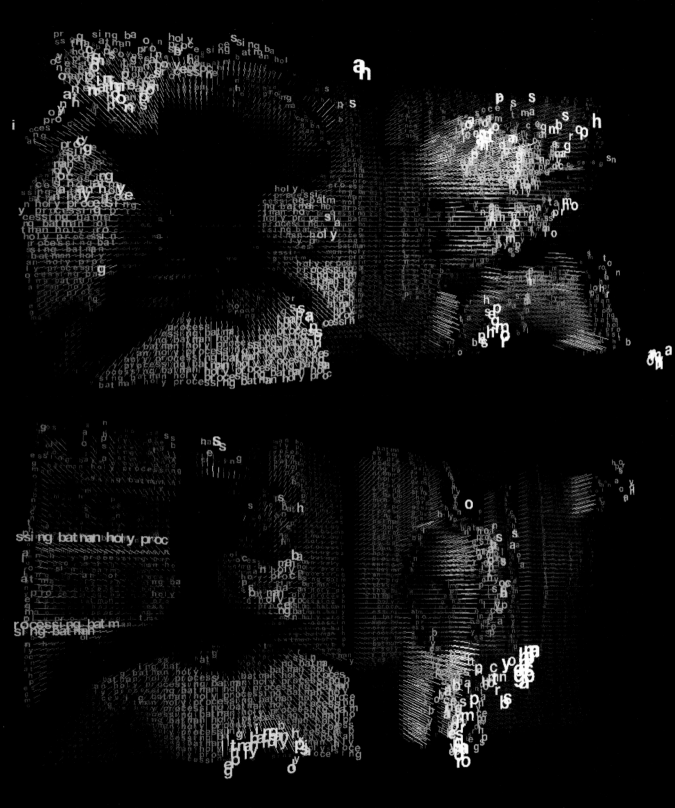

Holy typography, Batman! Robin and Batman go to the aid of Police Commissioner Gordon.

A scene from the opening titles after
being given a typographic treatment.

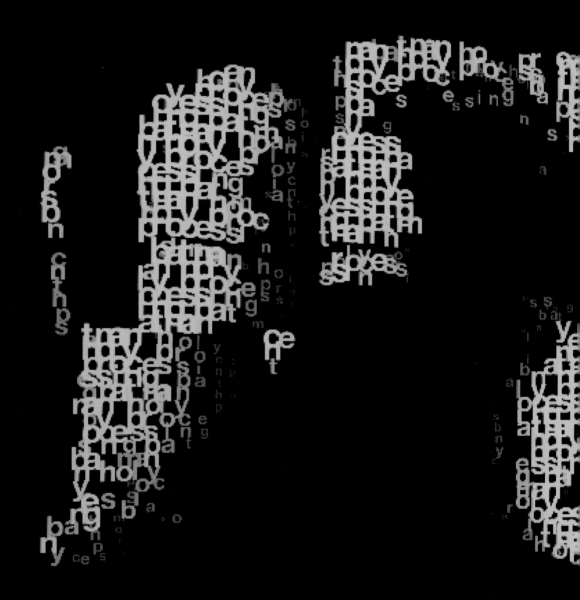

Somewhere in there is the Batmobile!

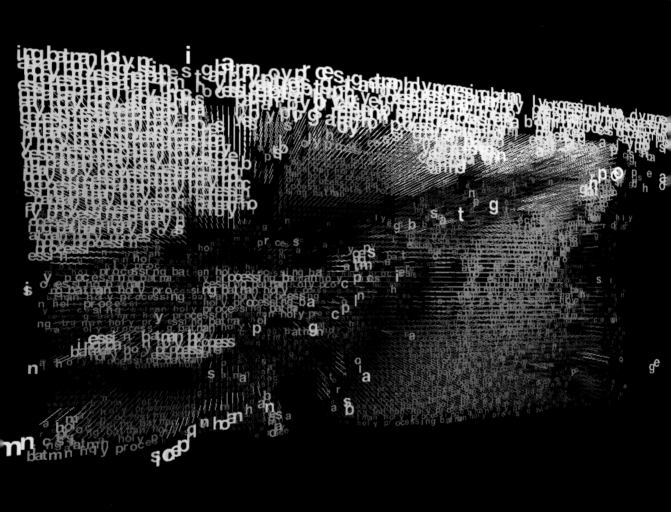

Catwoman taunts the Caped Crusader.

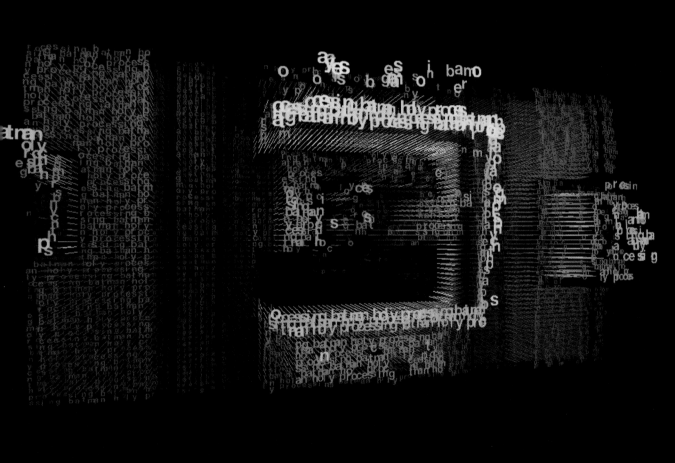

Now if you do a whole load of these images in sequence and then put them together using the "open as image sequence" in Apple's QuickTime Pro, you end up with a typographic interpretation of a film—or should that be a "TypoFilm"?

What has inspired the imaginations of more people than any other in this series is the concept I call "Cinema Redux." The basic premise is very simple: Can you distill a whole movie down to one image?

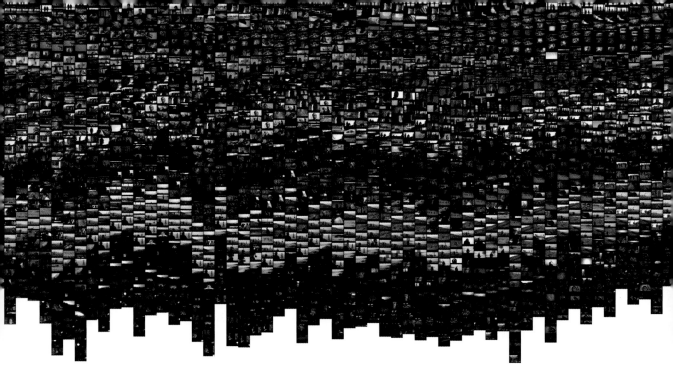

Of course, movies have sound information as well as visual, and we
can use the sound as we do pixels of a picture to influence our graphic
interpretation. Let's say we use volume to dictate how much of the
frames we see vertically, so loud passages show long parts of frames
and quiet passages show shorter parts. If we do that for the whole
film or portions of the film, we end up with a relationship between the
sound and the visual, with the sound shaping the look of our creation.
Here's what some of the 1971 film *Get Carter* looks like.

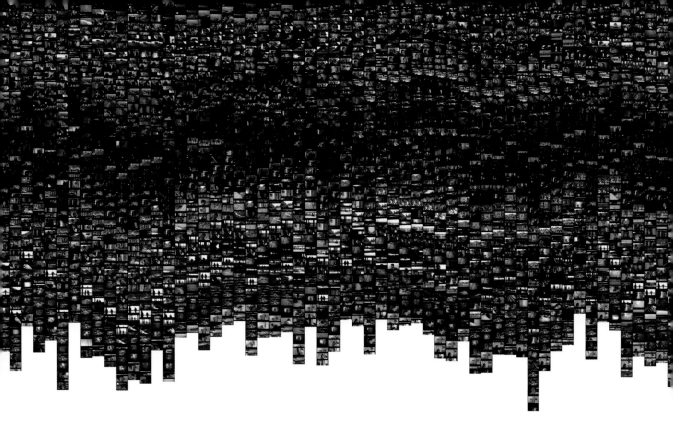

Sound information helps to dictate the final
composition from *Get Carter*.

Another variation is to use the same technique, but instead of butting up the images next to one another, place them in straight horizontal rows.

Joel and Ethan Coen's *The Man Who Wasn't There* now looks like some kind of DNA printout.

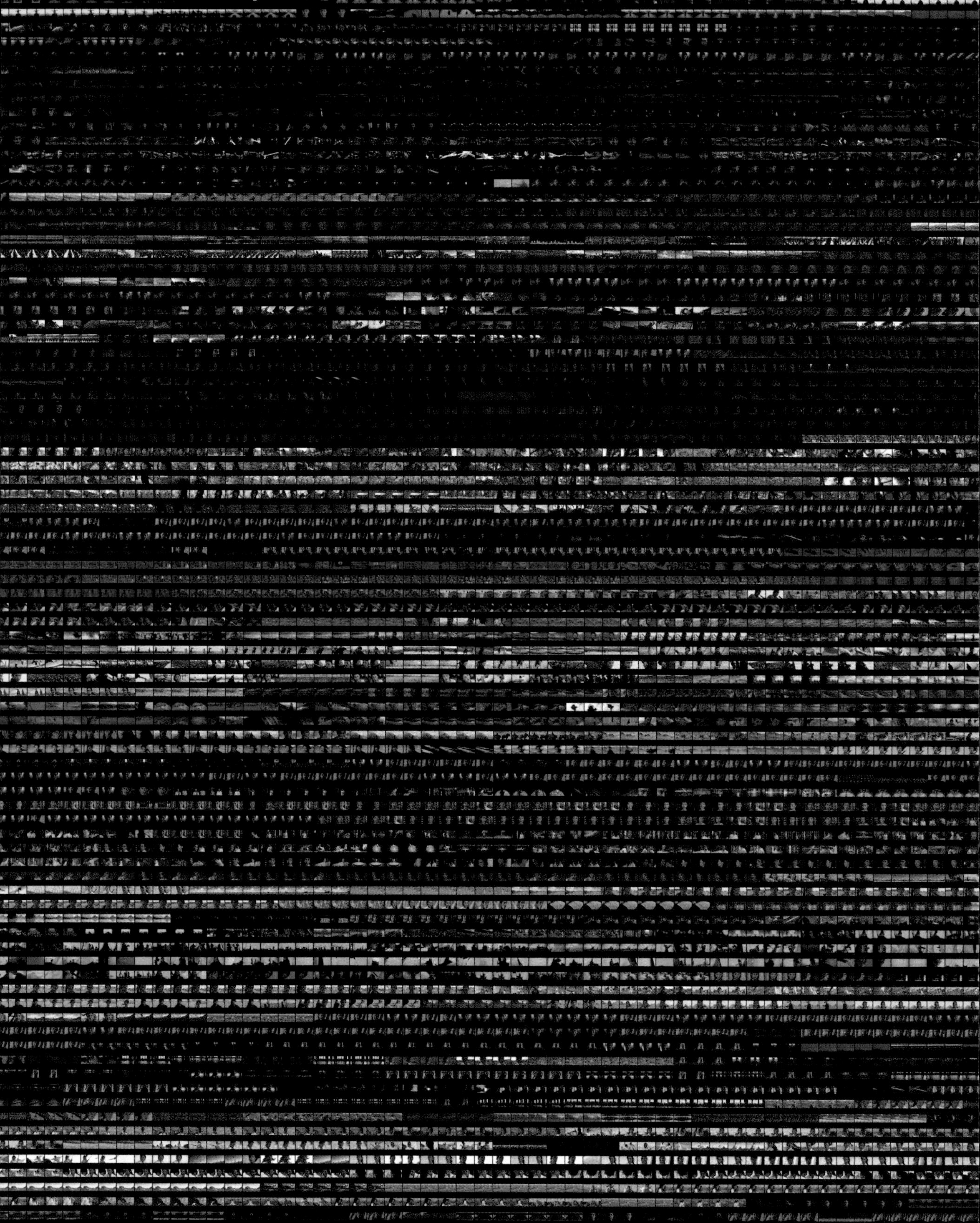

All these are iterations of the same basic idea—twisting the source DVD material into new interpretations, some more complex than others. But what has inspired the imaginations of more people than any other in this series is the concept I call "Cinema Redux." The basic premise is very simple: Can you distill a whole movie down to one image? I wrote a simple program in Processing that took one frame every second from a movie and rendered it out as an eight-by-six-pixel frame, repeating that for the entire movie, with each row representing one minute of film time. The end result was what I like to call "cinematic DNA." Bands of color appear within the movie and even show the rhythm of the editing process.

I want to point out that this Cinema Redux program took me no time at all to write; it's something like 50 lines of code. But that little piece of code, written to bring an initial idea to life, gave birth to a project that has since been featured on numerous blogs, and in countless magazines and books. The code itself is not clever in any way, shape, or form, but the end result got many people talking—not just geeks. And as far as I'm concerned, having that kind of social impact is what it's all about.

Many bands of color from Yimou Zhang's _Ying xiong (Hero)_.

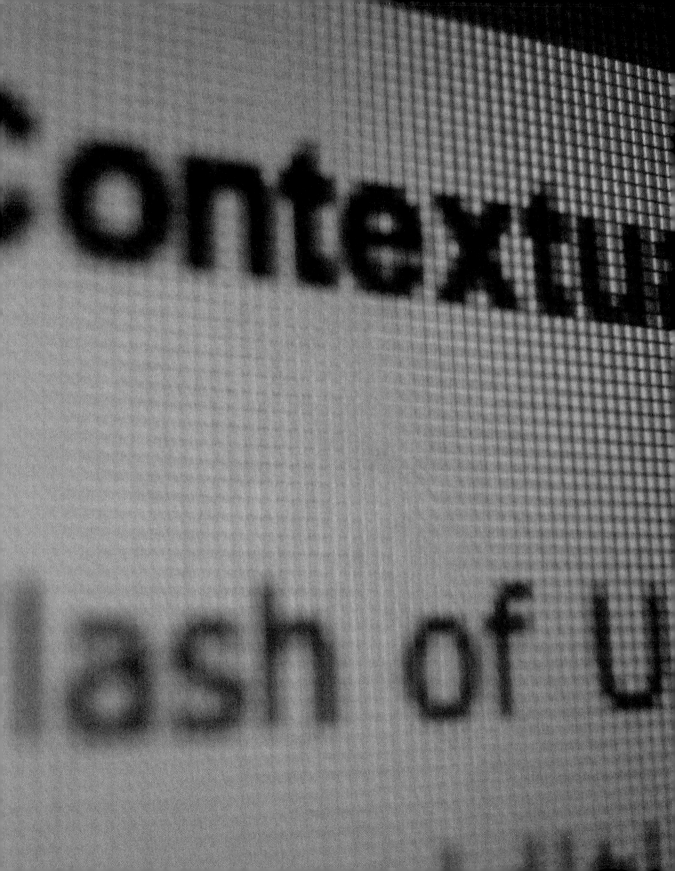

24

Contextual Memories

About two years ago, my wife, Lisa, and I were planning a holiday, look-ing around the Web at various holiday villas. As most people do, we bookmarked our favorites so we could come back to them at a later date. Yet when we wanted to go back to a specific villa—maybe the one with the 30-foot pool and the barbecue area—we were presented with a list of bookmarks that all said pretty much the same thing: "Villa in the South of France." There was no way of knowing which one of these many bookmarks was which without trawling through them all again.

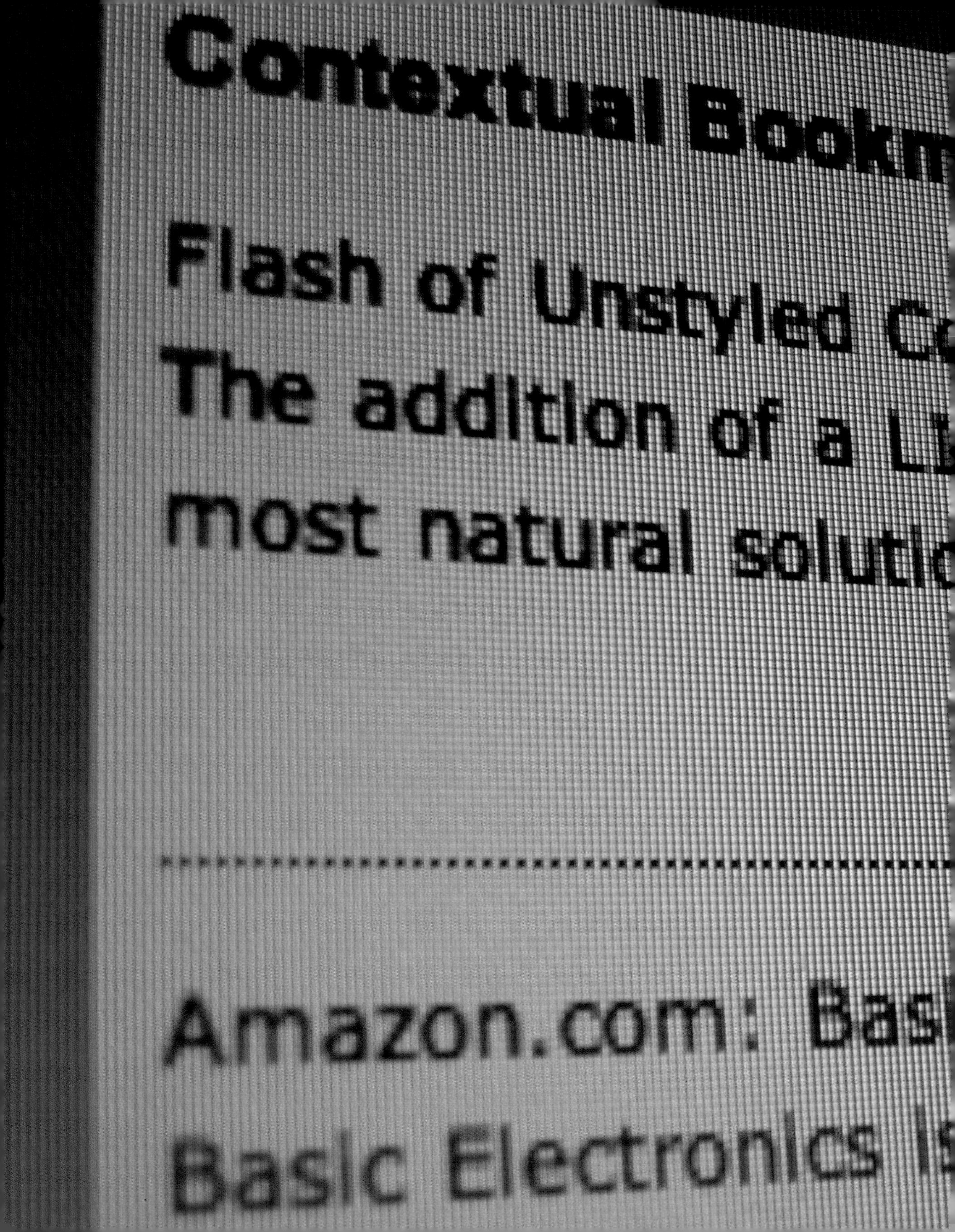

Contextual Bookm

Flash of Unstyled C
The addition of a Li
most natural solutio

Amazon.com: Bas

Basic Electronics is

Surely there's a better way to bookmark something by adding a bit of contextual information. After all, that's how we remember things: We jog our memories by trying to think of things linked to what we're trying to remember—what we were doing, who we were with.

I thought to myself, Surely there's a better way to bookmark something by adding a bit of contextual information, so that instead of looking at just the title of the page, you could also look at some appended text that would describe why you bookmarked it in the first place. After all, that's how we remember things: We jog our memories by trying to think of things linked to what we're trying to remember—what we were doing, who we were with, and the like.

But I always have a problem with the concept of adding this kind of metadata into a computer. It's a pain having to type stuff in, even just keywords; it's an extra step that I don't want to trouble people with. The thing with keywords is: You have to think some up! The very nature of metadata means that you have to add some keywords in order for there to be any for you to think of, if you get what I mean. To me, stuff like that always interrupts the user experience—the flow of how people are using what you made is suddenly disturbed and, personally, I don't like that to happen.

The flow and the rhythm of using something is to me one of the most important aspects of interaction design. What I wanted was something to capture context but not spoil the rhythm of surfing the Web.

Contextual Bookmark System Version

Flash of Unstyled Content (FOUC)
The addition of a LINK element to the bas
most natural solution to the FOUC problem

....

Amazon.com: Basic Electronics: Books
Basic Electronics is intended for students
electricity and electronics

The flow and the rhythm of using something is to me one of the most important aspects of interaction design. When you're using something that works well or just feels right, there's a rhythm or pace to your actions. And when that rhythm is interrupted suddenly, the pace of use is broken, and you have to get the rhythm up and running again. What I wanted was something to capture context but not spoil the rhythm of surfing the Web.

So how do you add metadata without requiring any typing or at least without making it any more painful for end users—in this case, just Lisa and me? Then it struck me that the information that would help us recall why we bookmarked something was staring us right in the face: the actual content of the site. What about creating something that allows you to select some text on the screen, click a button, and bingo! A bookmark is created with some nice contextual text—the very text you just selected. No typing. No thinking of words to type. For instance, we could select the sentence "includes beautiful roof terrace" right there on the page, and by clicking a button, the page would be bookmarked along with that helpful little bit of memory-jogging text.

Using a little bit of JavaScript, I created what people term a "bookmarklet." These are basically little bits of canned scripts that can sit in your browser tool bar and do pretty much anything that you can do with JavaScript. It's like writing a tiny piece of software that just sits in the browser window waiting to be activated. Here's what the code looked like:

```
javascript:x=escape(getSelection());window.location='http://
➥www.brendandawes.com/jotter/index.php?text='+x+'&url='+
➥document.location+'&title='+document.title;
```

Helpful Site

Learn how bookmarklets work:

http://en.wikipedia.org/wiki/
Bookmarklet

Essentially what's happening here is that the code grabs a user's selected text from a Web page and then sends that text, together with the Web page URL and title, to a PHP script. That script then passes that information into a database (MySQL).

It worked like a charm for us, generating a constantly growing page of bookmarks, complete with extra helpful information for each, accessible no matter where we are in the world. To be honest, it didn't make it any easier to trawl the Web for holiday accommodations because of the large amount of information you get back from search engines these days. But at least we had a better system for bookmarking things we liked; a system that would work on any site that had selectable text—which is pretty much every HTML site!

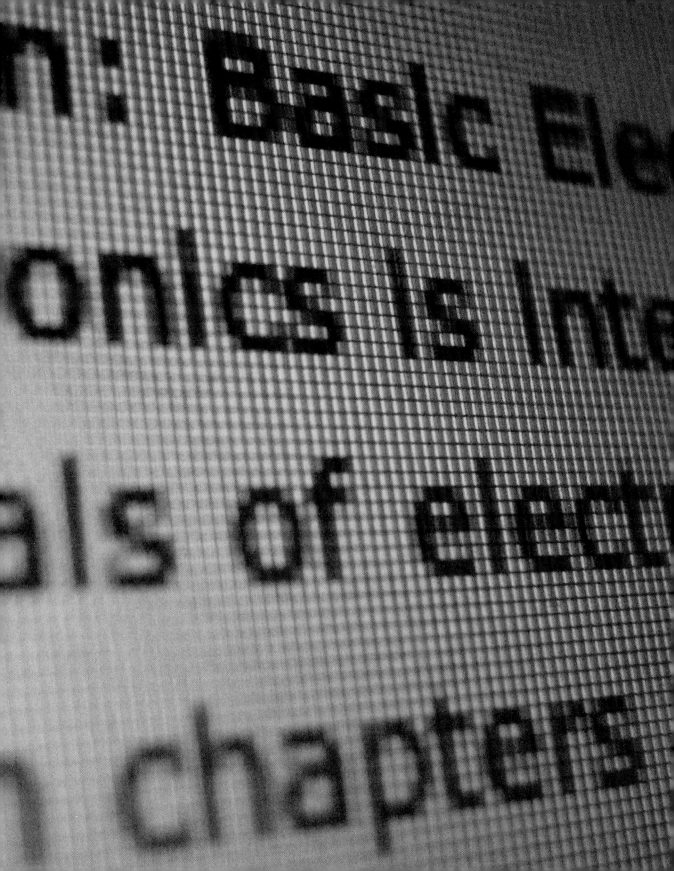

Whilst this little project used three different technologies—JavaScript, PHP, and MySQL—each bit was really simple to make. The key was thinking about how people use their memories and remember things. That's what helped me to look at the problem from a different angle and then find a technological solution to solving it.

obably the

2006-01-26

25

Rock 'n' Roll

Probably the first video game I ever played was the classic Defender, made by Williams Electronics back in the '80s. The game scared a lot of people because of the complexity of its controls—there were loads of buttons together with a vertical joystick—and to play the game well, you had to master all of them. But once you did, it was very rewarding.

Watch anybody play a video game. It's not just their heads and hands that control the interaction; their entire bodies are immersed in the experience.

Essentially the game was a sideways-scrolling shoot-'em-up in which you controlled a spaceship trawling a landscape to rescue people from the alien attackers, who came in waves. Once you got past the early stages, the game quickly became insane as you tried to save people and kill thousands of enemy hoards at the same time. And the sound, unlike any other in the arcade, heightened the tension and plunged you even further into the action. After playing a long session, you pretty much felt exhausted, like some video athlete.

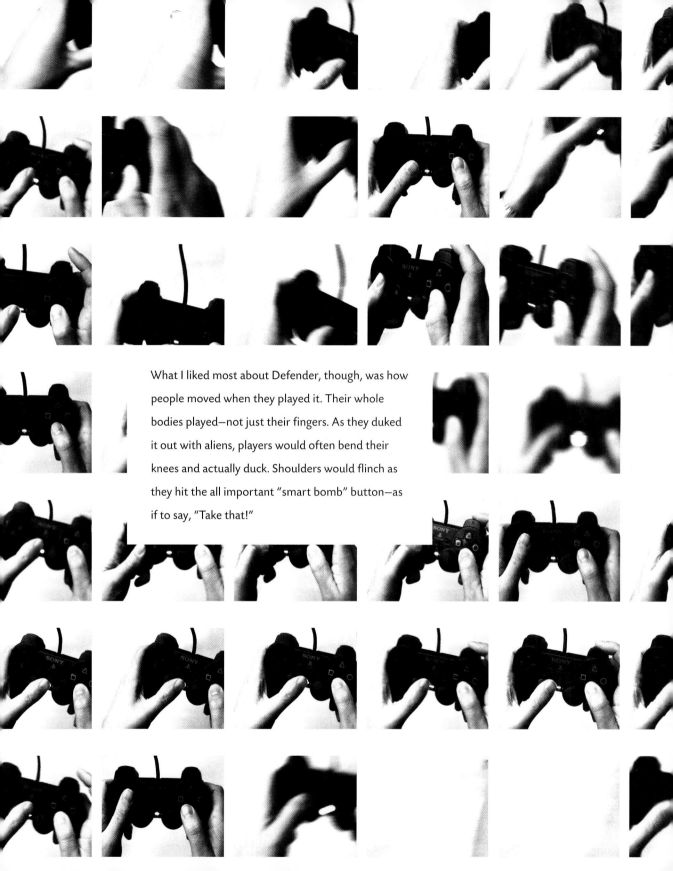

What I liked most about Defender, though, was how people moved when they played it. Their whole bodies played—not just their fingers. As they duked it out with aliens, players would often bend their knees and actually duck. Shoulders would flinch as they hit the all important "smart bomb" button—as if to say, "Take that!"

Since then I've always been fascinated watching people play games on PlayStation 2 and other consoles. Especially driving games. Watch anybody play a driving game and they will literally "swerve" around corners using their whole body. It's not just their heads and hands that control the interaction; their entire bodies are immersed in the experience.

As this time lapse of me playing the crazy driving game Burnout 3 demonstrates, I'm not just steering the analog joystick with my thumb; I'm actually tilting the whole joy pad side to side. Game players just do this naturally, although it has no bearing on the game at all.

So it's nice to see that companies such as Nintendo have recognized the importance of these physical idiosyncrasies and are building the action of tilting and swaying into the new generation of game controllers like those of Nintendo Revolution. Observing human behavior, rather than just the output or results of interactions on a screen, can lead to new iterations and innovations. And maybe they will finally improve my game play!

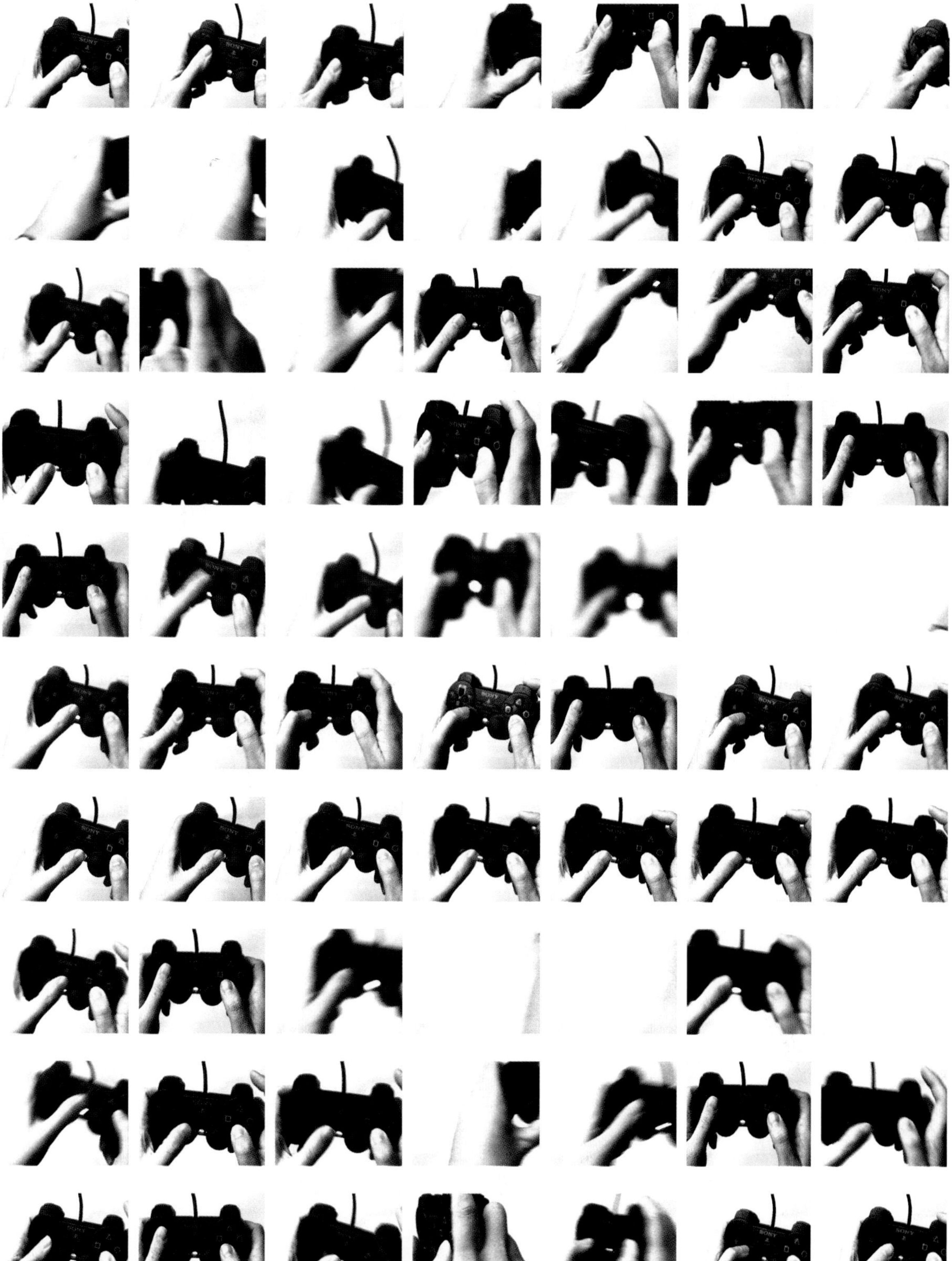
SONY

the times,
and info fo
reunions...
keep tunin

26

Mariah Carey Syndrome

Many years ago at a Flashforward conference in London, I first talked about what I termed the "Mariah Carey Syndrome." For the majority of you who weren't in the audience at that time, here's the lowdown on what I meant, and why I still feel it's important to talk about.

One of the first Flash sites I built was a full-on text-and-circle fest—words and phrases flying in from all directions and circles going from small to big before your very eyes. This was the Mariah Carey Syndrome in full force.

soon...

Mariah Carey has something like an eight-octave range. You've got to admit, that's pretty impressive. She can sing notes way down low and then hit the very high ones, seemingly without blinking one of those perfectly formed eyes. But my problem is this: Just because she has that ability doesn't mean she has to use it on all the notes of all her songs!

I, for one, find it painful that just one word can't be sung normally. Instead we must endure each word being thrown up and down several octaves. Why? Because she can.

Now I have a confession: I suffered from Mariah Carey Syndrome. The rationale of doing something just because you can is actually used often in design, including—and I'm very guilty here—the early uses of Flash.

When Flash first appeared on the scene, Web users were inundated with text flying all over the place. A word could no longer be just a word—it had to take wing and soar. A sentence could no longer just be placed on the screen. Oh no. Now that we had the ability to fly text in, we developers were going to use it on everything—and I mean everything. (It kind of reminds me of that band name "We've Got a Fuzzbox and We're Going to Use It.") And because of that, Flash started to get a bad rap. Suddenly we were lost in a digital sea of Skip Intros, long-winded animations, and full-screen extravaganzas.

And yeah, as I said, I'm guilty as charged. One of the first Flash sites I built was a full-on text-and-circle fest—words and phrases flying in from all directions and circles going from small to big before your very eyes. This was the Mariah Carey Syndrome in full force: using the new-found power of a cool box of tricks just because you can, with no regard for whether it has any meaning or purpose. But you know what? That site won a top design award! It just goes to show how crazy the whole industry was back then, and how design was being seduced by the technology rather than technology being used in the service of good design.

Though that site is no longer live, I still keep it on my hard drive as an example of what not to do. Looking back on this early work is pretty embarrassing, but I don't actually regret any of it. Why? Because as part of the process of experimentation and exploration, you have to go through your Mariah Carey period in order to come out the other side a better designer.

Historically when any new technology comes out, users of the new toys it brings go pretty mad with it. Take sampling back in the eighties, when it suddenly became affordable. The first really big use of sampling then was Paul Hardcastle's dance track "19." Sampling a documentary about the Vietnam War, Hardcastle then fused it with an electro-pop backing track and created an almost entirely new genre of music. After that came a million records sampling and mixing anything and everything from dog barks to diesel engines to other artists' sounds.

It was an awful period for music in one sense, but completely necessary for the evolution of sampling techniques. Did sampling disappear overnight because of these "bad" uses of new technology? Of course not. As people got to know the technology better, their use of it became more subtle and focused. There's probably not a recording made today that doesn't employ some form of sampling. Be it classical, pop, rock, hip hop, or whatever, they all use some form of sampling technology—even if it's just the process of recording a single note digitally.

The same has happened with Flash—it's now become a much more sophisticated tool for delivering truly great experiences to the end user. But each time I begin to use it, I remember Mariah Carey and wonder if, just because I have these great features at my fingertips, every pixel needs to be drowned in them.

Next time you're cranking up a new piece of technology, though, I say do a total Mariah Carey—go for broke, push and prod every button, see what it can do and where it can take you. But from time to time, just ask yourself, *That fuzzbox—I've got it, but do I need to use it?*

27

From Thin Air

As I write this, there are bits of data flowing around my network. In the background, my email is being checked every 20 minutes, and any Web browser I have open might be pulling in dynamic data to update a feed or pull in a new advertisement.

This all goes on unseen by us. But by employing what we call *packet sniffers*—software that can monitor traffic on a network—we can use that normally invisible source to create visual representations of digital traffic.

By taking a special ready-made code library called Carnivore and knocking something together in Processing, I was able to see the raw ASCII text of what was flying around the network.

Following pages: The basic ASCII text returned when surfing the BBC news Web site. The odd font size difference is just a glitch in the software, which I left in.

Opposition urge Clarke to resign   </a>   <br 7>   </div>

.stm"><img height="66" hspace="0" align="left" vspace="3" border="0" width="66" alt="" src="ht
wsimg.bbc.co.uk/media/images/41608000/jpg/_41608434_blair6666.jpg" /></a>   <img height="66"
"0" align="left" vspace="0" border="0" width="5" alt="" src="http://newsimg.bbc.co.uk/shared/i
f
<div class="arr">   <a href=
uk_politics/4946988.stm">   Foreign prisoners: The numbers   </a>
9   <div class="arr">
<div class="arr">   <a href="/1/hi/uk_politics/4945046.stm">   Prof
arles Clarke   </a>   </div>   ef="/1/hi/uk_politics/4945046.stm">   Prof
Profile: Charles Clarke   </a>   </div>

<div   c l   <div class="arr">   <a href="/1/hi/uk/4939376.s
i/   9006 3 ipp://1   179   <a h
= "#" onclick = "launchAVConsoleV3((nin_depth/uk/2006/deportation
a href="#" onclick="_row')"><img height="13" haunchAVConsoleV3('in_depth/uk/space="0" align=
vsp2006/deportation_row');a"=<"i2m"g bhoeridgehrt=="01"3 "w ihdstpha=c"e6=0 "0 "a latl=i"g
lce=f"th"t tvps:p/a7cnee=w"s2i"m gb.obrbdce.rc=o".00 6 width="60" alt="" src="http://newsing.b
k/nok/nol/shared/img/v3/videonews.gif" />Reports and interviews</a>   / shared / i m g
videonews.gif " /> R<pborr tcsl eaanrd= "ianltle"r v/i>ews < / a >
6 4 0   < br clear = all >
width = "203" 3   6 4 0   = "0" vspace = "3" border =
<div class="arr">   <a href="http://news.bbc.co.uk/1/hi/in_depth/uk/200
ns/default.stm">   In-depth: Prisons in the UK   </a>   <div height=
ace="0" vspace="3" border="0" width="203" alt="" src="http://news   <div class="rr">   e 3 ipp
168.2.22:631/printers/_4300_Series "Brendan Dawes   s Computer" "4300 Series" "4300 Series" d00
p://192.168.2.11:631/printers/_4300_Series "Ba   <div clas
<a href="</a1 /hhrie7fu=k"_/p1o/lhiit/iucks_/p4o9l4i9t8i7c8s./s4t9m4"9>8 7 8 .
R o b b e r i e_sR oubpb e6r%i ebsu tu pc r6i%m eb ustt acbrliem e
b l e </a>   </a>   < br   />   </div>

s<sd=i"va rcrl"a>s s = "arr"<>a   h r e f = "</a1 /hhrie/fu=k"_/p1o/lhiit/iuuc__politics/
.stm">   s/4950238.stm">   SSttaanndaardds ss qquueesstiioon
veerr PPrreesscccoottt
ddiivv>>   < /li
li>   <li><a href="https://ssl.bbc.co.uk/syndication/html/registration/" title="Access BBC N
dlines free from your site" class="none">Headlines for your site</a></li>   <ul>   <ul id="cop
top>   <li class="copyright"><a href="http://news.bbc.co.uk/1/hi/help/3281849.stm" title="BBC
ight Notice">BBC Copyright Notice</a></li>   <li class="backtotop"><a href="#top" title="">Ba
op</a></li>   </ul>   <ul id="footnav">   <li>   a 41006 3 ipp://192.168.2.22:631/printers/Blue
odem "Brendan Dawes   s Computer" "Bluetooth-Modem" "Fax Printer"   !-- story sport logo in ban
ry sport logo in bannerr---->   <map name="bbc_sport_story"   <map name="bbc_sport_story" id=
cb_cs_psoprotr_ts_tsotroyr"y>"   <a<raeraeea_alt="bbc sport" coords=".1,1,119.34" href="http
bbc alt="bbc sport" coords=".1,1,119.34" href="http://news.bbc.co.uk/" />   </map>   <!-- stor c
>   </map>   <!-- story watch/listen in banner-->   <map name="banner_watchlisten" atch/liste
anner-->   <map name="banner_watchlisten" id="banner_waid="banner_watchlisten"ch h Vasrteean
=<"awraetac ha llti=sr"watch listen" coords=".0,6,201.33" href="javascript: void re"n" coords=

SN. uu Lwnrk Slorage Link ror u.upnp-LinksysNetwork SLUUSDZ.0 DISKS-1 NIS.SSup-aLrrugE Lin
USB2.0 Disks-00045A0FC24D::urn:schemas-upnp-org   SERVER: Linux/2.4.22-xfs, UPnP/1.0, Intel SDK
dPenvPi cdee:vNiectewso r/k1 .S2t.o rUaSgNe: Luiunikd: fuoprn pU-SLBi2n.k0s.yDSi.sNkest:w1o r
tor aNgOeT ILFiYn k" fHoTrT PU/S1B.21.0 HDOiSsTk:s -203090.4255A50.F2C5254.D=5:0:ur1n9:0s
CmAaCsH-Eu-pCnOpN-ToRrOgL:.d emvaixc-ea:gNee=t1w8o0r k LSOtCoArTaIgOeN l ihntkt pf:o/r/ 1U9S2
0 0 .D2i .s7k7s-:617 8 9 /dHhTtTtPp/:1/./0w w4w0.4w 3N.ootr gF/oTuRn/dR ECCo-nhttennlt4-0T/ylpoe
.edxttd/"h>t ml   <<h!tdmolc>t y p<eh ehatdm>l< tpiutbllei>c4 0"4- /"/ WP3aCg/e/ DNToDt HFTo
4<./0t iTtrlaen>s i t i o</nlailn/k/ EtNy"p e="h"ttttepx:t///cwswsw". wr3e.lo=p"ss/tyTyRl/eRsEhCe-
lh4r0e/fl=o"o/sseh.adrtedd"/>e r ror</hctsmsl/>e r r<ohre.acds>s<"t i"t>l e >4 0"4-/h ePa
N<obto dFyo umnadr<ag/itnnihtelieg>h t = 0<"l imnakr gtiynpwei=d"tthe=xt/0"c sstso"p mraerrgi
leftmargin="0">   <div id="error">   <img =lr"stylesheet" href="/shared/erc="http://newsimg.
.uk/shar ror/css/error.css">   </head>   <body marginheight="0"   marg error/img/bbc_news_spo
Y" HTTP/1.1 HOST: 239.0 USB2.0 Disks-00045A0FC245:5:.u2r5nS:.s2c5h0e:m1a9s0-0u p nCpA-CoHrEg-
89/device.xml NT: urn:schemasOTIFY HTTP/1.1 HOST: 239.255.25uSp.5-0o:r1g9:0d00e v iCcAeC:
CWo0nNrTkR OSLt:o rmaagxe-aLgien=k1.8f0o r LUOSCBA2T.:0 Disks:1 ssdPIa0lcN: http://192.1
7:6789/devifive SERVER: Linux/2.4.22-xfe.xml NT: urn:schems,UPnP/1.0, Intel SDK for UPnP dev
1.2 USN: uuid:upnp-LinksysNetwork Storage Link for USB2.0 Disks-a0-upnp-org:device:Network
e Link for USB2.0 Disks:1 NTk045A0FC24D::urn:schemas-upnp-org:device:Network Storage Link: ssd
e SERVER: Linux/2.4.22-xfs, UPnP/1.0, Intel SDK for UPnP devi for USB2.0 Disks:1   ces/
SN: uuid:upnp-LinksysNetwork Storage Link for USB2.0 Disks-00045A0FC24D::urn:schemas-upnp-org:
-Network Storage Link for USB2.0 Disks:1   GET /0.gif?-RS-News-RS-t-RS-HighWeb_Story
S-4945922-RS-p-RS-39099-RS-a-RS-Domestic-RS-u-RS-/1/hi/uk_politics/4945922.stm-RS-r-RS-(none)-R
--RS-z-RS-18-RS- HTTP/1.1 Accept: */* Accept-Language: en-us Accept-Encoding: gzip, deflate
- BBCNewsAudience=Domestic; BBC-UID=34e2a6f1b11603f7f48ba9af5158c8c4ddf91f51805840e052e02c85a9
0Mozilla/f25%2e0%20%28Macintosh%3b%20U%3b%20PPC%20Mac%200S%3b%20X%3b%20en%2dus%29%20AppleWebKHTTP/
0 OK Date: Thu, 27 Apr 2006 12:52:21 GMT Server: Apache Last-Modified: Wed, 22 Mar 2006 11:2
MT Etag: "2b-a8b6bd00" Accept-Ranges: bytes Content-Length: 43 Cache-Control: max-age=2 Ex
Thu, 27 Apr 2006 12:52:23 GMT Keep-Alive: timeout=10, max=153 Connection: Keep-Alive Conten
image/gif GIF89a   D 9006 3 ipp://192.168.2.22:631/printer
us_C64 "Brendan Dawes   s Computer" "Stylus C64" "EPSON C64 Series (1.1) 9006 3 ipp://192.168.
317printers/Stylus_C64 "Brendan Dawes   s Computer" "Stylus C64" "EPSON C64 Series (1.1)" d00e
e3 ipp://192.168.2.11:631/printers/_4300_Series "Brendan Dawes   s Computer" "4300 Series" "4300 Serie
ies" 41006 3 ipp://192.168.2.22:631/printers/Bluetooth-M9006 3 ipp://192.168.2.22:631/printers/
C64 "Brendan Dawes   s Computer" "Stylus B6uendan Dawes   s Computer" "Stylu4" "EPSON C64 Seri
I)" 9006 3 ipp://192.168.2.11:631/pr iCC64" "EPSON C64 Series et(r1s./15)"t y l4e1t0o0o6t h3- Mi
m//"1B9r2ee.n1d6a8n. 2D.a1w1e:s6 3 1 /spr Cionmtpeurrts"e/rB"l u=eBtlouoettho-oMtohmd-eMmo d"eBmr"
aanx DParwienst e r's Computer" "Bluetooth-Modem" "Fax Printer" 41006 3 ipp://192.168.2.22
rinters/Internal_Modem "Brendan Dawes   s Computer" "Internal_Modem" "Fax Printer" 41006 3 ipp
3 ipp://192.168.2.22:631/printers/Stylus_C64 "Brendan Dawes   s Computer" "Stylus C64" "EPSON
168.2.11:631/printers/Internal_Modem "Brendan Dawes   s Computer" "Internal_Modem" "Fax Printer
ries (1.1)" 9006 3 ipp://192.168.2.11:6317printers/Stylus_C64 "Brendan Dawes   s Computer" "Sty
4" "EPSON C64 Series (1.1)"   & SMB   d   #   # SMB
d   d00e 3 ipp://192.168.2.22:631/printers/_4300_Series "Brendan Dawes   s Computer" "4300
0 "4300 Series" d00e 3 ipp://192.168.2.11:631/printers/_4300_Series "Brendan Dawes   s Computer
0 Series" "4300 Series"   www.apple.com   www.apple.com
w apple com akadns net + -   p   [=   checkip dyndns org   [=   che
yndns org   2   3   ?   3   5   3   3 SP 41006 3 ipp://192.168.2.22:63
ters/Bluetooth-Modem "Brendan Dawes   s Computer" "Bluetooth-Modem" "Fax Printer" 41006 3 ipp:
8.2.11:631/printers/Bluetooth-Modem "Brendan Dawes   s Computer" "Bluetooth-Modem" "Fax Printe
ers/_4300_Series "Brendan Dawes   s Computer" "4300 Series" "4300 Series" d00e 3 ipp://192.168.
31/printers/_4300_Series "Brendan Dawes   s 0Computer" "4300 Series" "4300 Computer "4300 Seri
300 Seroeries HTTP/1.1 200 OK Co no-cache Pragma: no-cache Content-Length: 104   <html><he
tle>Current IP Chtent-Type: text/html Server: DynDNS-CheckIP/0.2 Connect eck</title></head><h
lose Cache-Control: no-yc>aCcuurrenntPtr aIgPm aAd:dnroe-scsa:c h8e2. 4C2o.n1t15e1n.18-6L<e/
hs:> <1/0h4t m1 > < hh tml><head><title>Current IP Check</title></head><bodv>Current IP Addr

Helpful Sites

The Carnivore library for Processing:

http://rhizome.org/carnivore/
processing.php

The home of Processing:

www.processing.org

Hmmm. How about if we take each letter, find out its ASCII code value, and then abstract that number to dictate the size and shade of boxes? Move around the BBC news site and voilà—incidental image creation made just by surfing around a Web site.

A little iteration created with the same raw source.

The BBC site never looked so good!

What, no AC/DC!!

Average Rating: ★★★★½

Total: 3 songs

Put The Beatles On ITunes!

Average Rating: ★★★★½

Total: 8 songs

ITunes Need Led Zeppelin...

Average Rating: ★★★★½

28

Bending the Rules

I always find it gratifying when a new technology or system comes out and then users distort it into something else, usually for their own means or to make it much more useful than the makers ever envisaged. The classic example is mobile phone text messaging, which is huge here in the U.K. and across Europe. Short Message System, or SMS, was originally invented so engineers could send quick messages back and forth. It was never meant for mass public use—nobody thought that ordinary people would use it. But then the public found out about it and guess what? Ordinary people *do* find it very useful. So average users ended up taking the technology and making it work for them.

There is a budding movement on the iTMS site: People have started to use their own iMixes as an impromptu way to protest or campaign for their favorite bands on iTunes.

ADIOHEAD on itune

ge Rating: ★★★★★

16 songs

he Red Hot Chilis on

ge Rating: ★★★★★

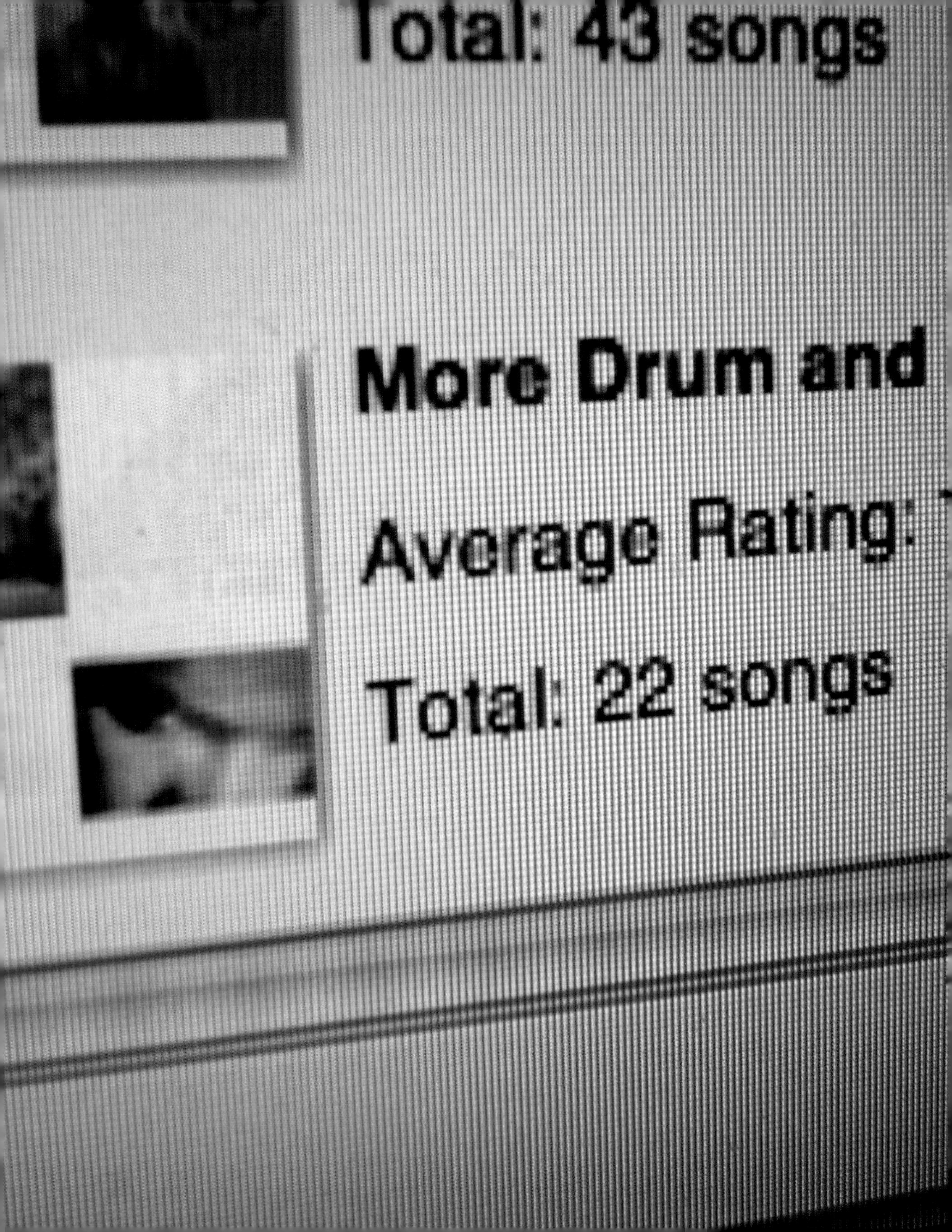

Total: 43 songs

More Drum and

Average Rating:

Total: 22 songs

At the moment, I like what is happening at the iTunes Music Store. No doubt you already know that people can create what Apple calls an "iMix," which is basically a digital version of the old-school mix tape—one person's favorite compilation of songs that he or she creates for friends or other people to enjoy. And while there are indeed many such iMixes on the iTMS site, there is also a budding movement there: People have started to use their own iMixes as an impromptu way to protest or campaign for their favorite bands on iTunes.

At the time of this writing, the top three–rated iMixes are "What, no AC/DC!!"; "Put The Beatles on iTunes!!!"; and "iTunes Need Led Zeppelin." So here's a system originally created for people to publish their own digital mix tapes that is now being used as a quick and dirty digital petition! Now that's rock 'n' roll!

29

Evidence of Use

Something I'm constantly wrestling with in the arena of digital media is its lack of evidence that a digital artifact has been "touched," outside of information like "last modified date" and the like. There's no way of showing visually that something has been used—a ten-year-old file icon looks exactly the same as it did when it was created. A digital photo looks as pristine as the day it was taken. After all, isn't that what makes digital images so great—the fact that they don't degrade with time unless they get turned into "analog" prints? Of course the answer is, "Yes." But is anyone asking the question, What are we losing in this super clean, time-irrelevant medium? Do people *want* to see evidence of use?

The page has a story impregnated into it, a narrative that has been permanently stuck to it. Because that's what paper pages can do— they acquire signs of use and accidents that tell a future reader something about what they meant to someone.

As I'm typing away at home, I'm surrounded by lots of personal stuff, some from my early childhood. Here's the very first copy of *Computer & Video Games*, from 1981. It was probably this very magazine that got me into the creative use of computers. But look at it. The pages are faded, the corners battered, and there are even tea stains on the advertisement for the ZX81. Now just stop a moment. The ZX81 was my very first computer. A glorious 1K of RAM. This was the machine that got me hooked on programming and the possibilities of computing, and you could say that was a defining moment in my life. And here's the document to prove it. The tea stains suggest that I was looking over this two-page ad for quite a while, or at least that I kept coming back to it. And there in the little order form section, I've optimistically written down the price of the bits I'd love to own!

Available n

the ZX Printe

for only £49.95

Designed exclusively for use with
the ZX81 (and ZX80 with 8K BASIC
ROM), the printer offers full alpha
erics and highly sophistic
cial feature is
xactly wh

The tea stains suggest that I was looking over this two-page ad for quite a while, or at least that I kept coming back to it.

The page has a story impregnated into it, a narrative that has been permanently stuck to it. Because that's what paper pages can do—they acquire signs of use and accidents that tell a future reader something about what they meant to someone. And that is very, very important. This page is now personal to me—that is my story on that page. It gives me a jumping off point to wax lyrical about what the ZX81 meant to me in a much more meaningful way than, say, a *JPEG* of a ZX81 could ever do.

Now compare that to how I now buy similar bits of kit. My first iPod, for instance. I have no such historical document of buying it because it was bought online. I can tell you now about how I would trawl for hours on the Web, reading everything I could about the iPod. Like looking longingly through a shop window, I would sit there with my cup of tea thinking of the day I would own one. Of course, you'll have to take my word for this because I have nothing to prove it. There are no tea stains on the Apple Web site from several years ago and anyway, that version of the Apple site has gone for good. There's nothing for me to attach my memories to. Nothing that says, "This was the moment I saw my first iPod." Of course, I still have my first iPod, and it does show evidence of use. It's battered beyond belief, full of scratches and marks from being dropped, but that's because—hey, it's a physical object!

There are no tea stains on the Apple Web site from several years ago and anyway, that version of the Apple site has gone for good. There's nothing for me to attach my memories to. Nothing that says, "This was the moment I saw my first iPod."

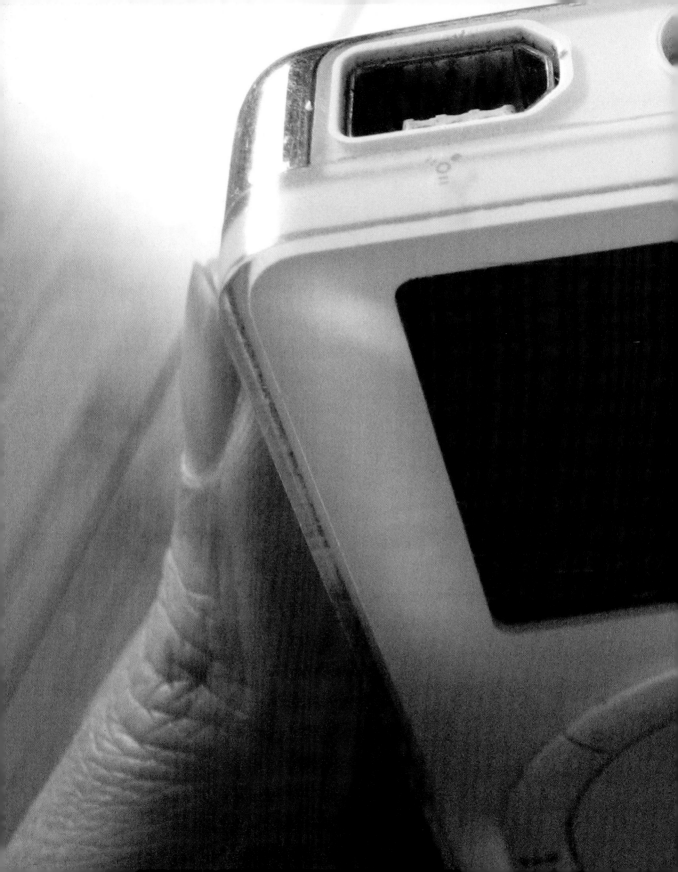

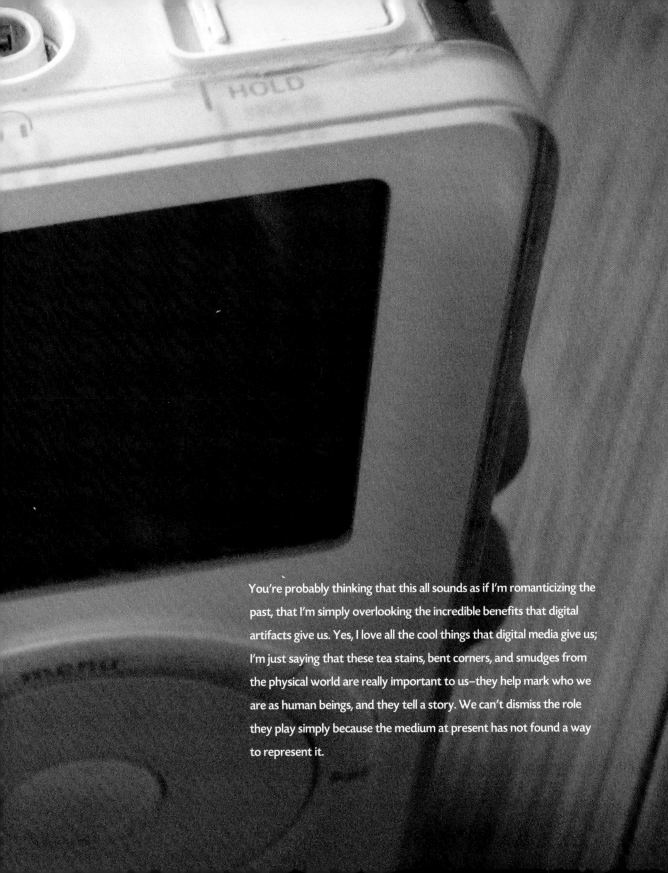

You're probably thinking that this all sounds as if I'm romanticizing the past, that I'm simply overlooking the incredible benefits that digital artifacts give us. Yes, I love all the cool things that digital media give us; I'm just saying that these tea stains, bent corners, and smudges from the physical world are really important to us—they help mark who we are as human beings, and they tell a story. We can't dismiss the role they play simply because the medium at present has not found a way to represent it.

Digital photography and digital images really need this. Photographs are all about capturing a still moment in time, yet does it not leave you a little cold when you look at digital images on your screen? There's absolutely no sense of time or narrative infused into the photo itself unless, of course, you print it out—and then it becomes an analog artifact rather than a digital one.

The online photo-sharing site Flickr.com goes some way toward letting digital photos take on these narrative scratches in time. For instance, you can see how many times a photo has been viewed, together with comments that people have left after viewing it. There's also a note system, so you can leave actual notes on the photo itself—kind of like writing on the back of a printed photograph. People love to know this stuff. They love to see how many times their photo has been viewed or whether it's been set as a favorite by someone. In a small way, this is evidence of use by friends, family, and people you don't know. When you come back to this photo a few months down the line, things have been added, which in turn adds to the story of the photo.

Digital is a fantastic medium full of incredible features such as portability, storage capacity, and a consistent state of newness. But I really think there's room to merge some of the touchy-feely stuff from the analog world into the digital world. After all, those accidents, those little scratches, those moments in time are some of the things that separate us from the machines.

30

Comfortably Numb

Is it just me, or does everything these days seem rather, well, pleasant? It seems that we're living in a time where we celebrate the ordinary, the safe, and the status quo.

Strangely enough, as I approach the age of 40, I seem to be a lot more rebellious than I was as a kid. So much so that I question things all the time—sometimes silly, trivial things, such as those little supermarket "batons" on the conveyer belt at the cashier's stand that are meant to separate your shopping items from those of the person behind you in line. We never used to have those things and somehow everybody managed to shop perfectly well without them. But now just try not putting that baton down—you're seen as a maverick, a subversive who won't conform to the way it has to be! The invention of that baton is all part of the "pleasant" world we now live in. Well, I say we need more people saying "no" to those pesky little batons!

One of my favorite movies of the last few years is Pixar's *The Incredibles*. I truly believe that film makes a statement about society today. We'd rather not have the odd individual with "super powers," thank you very much; we'd just like everyone to be the same. Or the flip side of that is: We want to make *everyone* feel super. That way nobody gets hurt or offended. Well, as the villain at the end of the film says, "When everyone is super, nobody is."

The fact is this: We need risk-takers in life. We need people who will stand up and say, "I'm going to do things another way." And creativity is absolutely about taking risks.

In regard to the creative process, "comfort" is a very nasty, horrible word. It's pretty much the cancer of creativity, and you can see when it gets hold of people and doesn't let go

In regard to the creative process, comfort is a very nasty, horrible word. It's pretty much the cancer of creativity, and you can see when it gets hold of people and doesn't let go. Look at what happened to Elvis. After all that early success, he became too comfortable to take risks anymore, and as a result his creative output plummeted. His body in the latter stages of his life epitomized his bloated comfort level. He wasn't hungry for success anymore; he was pretty much only hungry for burgers and peanut butter–and–banana sandwiches!

But at least Elvis changed things early on. Without him, rock 'n' roll might have taken a different path. What pains me more is when I get kids in for interviews who seem to have had all the life sucked out of them before they have even done anything. I can see in their eyes that comfort has them in its icy grip and they've started to give in. Their portfolios are pretty dull, mirroring everything else that's out there because that's safe—and besides, they got a top qualification on their degree course, so they must be good. But all they've really done is checked some easy-to-mark boxes. Well, the world doesn't need more box-checkers. We've got plenty of them already, and we actually need to start getting rid of some, not adding to the problem!

I get kids in for interviews who seem to have had all the life sucked out of them before they have even done anything. Their portfolios are pretty dull, mirroring everything else that's out there because that's safe.

Sir Christopher Wren, architect and risk-taker of the seventeenth century

History is full of people taking risks because they felt so passionate about changing things that they actually went out there and *did* change things, leaving behind lasting legacies. Some of them I've briefly mentioned in this book: John Whitney, Raymond Scott, the Zephyr skateboard team.

And of course, when I say history, I'm not just talking about the last 50 years or so. Just look at Christopher Wren, the architect of London's St Paul's Cathedral. The Anglican Church hated Wren's original design for the rebuilding of the cathedral. Wren had to go back and amend his plans so he could get the warrant design approved by the "client," who happened to be King Charles II. But because Charles II was a big fan of Wren's work, he wrote into the warrant a special clause that would "allow [Wren] the liberty in the Prosecution of his work, to make some variations, rather ornamental, than essential, as from Time to Time he should see proper." This was all that Wren needed to proceed with his original vision, not the one favored by the church. By the time the cathedral was completed, it bore pretty much no resemblance to the church-approved warrant design. With the support of his client, Wren took a massive risk, but it paid off because he knew his vision was right. He just had to bend the rules a little to get the result he wanted.

Creativity is not about playing safe, and it never should be. It should scare the hell out of you at times.
It should put you in uncomfortable places that challenge you at every step.